It's A

Raising Godly Children in Today's World

You're a Parent!

John Lehman

It's Apparent ... You're a Parent!
Raising Godly Children in Today's World

© John Lehman, 2013

Unless otherwise indicated, all Scripture quotations are from The Holy
Bible, English Standard Version® (ESV®), copyright © 2001 by Crossway, a
publishing ministry of Good News Publishers.
Used by permission. All rights reserved.

This (hardcover) edition: 978-0-9899532-0-7

Trade Paperback: 978-0-9899532-1-4

ePub: 978-0-9899532-2-1

MOBI: 978-0-9899532-3-8

PDF: 978-0-9899532-4-5

Typeset by Quinta Press (www.quintapress.com)

Published by www.GreatWriting.org, Greenville, South Carolina, USA,
info@GreatWriting.org

Cover design by www.GreatWriting.org

Printed in the USA

"Give me some tips on parenting" is not something I'd ask of many. I would of Lehman. I find it nearly impossible to read a book on parenting if I don't know the author's family. I do know Lehman's. That's why I found it impossible **not** to read this book. It reads as smoothly and pastorally as if he were your mentor across the coffee table, pouring into your life. Think of this practical and biblical book as strong morning coffee for the long day of parenting—with extra shots of Scripture.

Dave Hosaflook (Missionary to Albania)

John doesn't merely talk the talk—he walks the walk. This book isn't full of common-sense parenting, because biblical parenting is neither common nor natural. It demands supernatural wisdom and power.

Jeremy McMorris (From the Foreword)

The goal of this book is to help crystallize in parents' minds the importance of making the right choices for their children, and, through considering biblical principles that are laid out in God's Word, to please the Lord by the choices that are made and implanted.

Table of Contents

Foreword

Typically, an author would have someone better known than himself write a foreword to his book. For some strange reason, John has done the opposite, and I'm honored.

John Lehman has lived one of the best "sermons" I've ever seen. His life is truly exemplary in so many areas. His husbanding and parenting stand out above the rest, in my opinion.

John doesn't merely talk the talk—he walks the walk. Actually, he runs the run! John is a runner, and we've put in hundreds of miles together. On those miles, we've literally shed blood, sweat, and tears. Many of those miles "pounding the pavement" were spent discussing marriage and family issues. I was the recipient of a great deal of biblical wisdom over those miles. Many of those "Lehmanisms" have made their way into the McMorris home. I'm thankful that those "Lehmanisms" were profoundly biblical and profoundly practical. Things like, "Serve the Lord with gladness," "Drink water," "Enjoy the people you're with," and, "The pain of the punishment must outweigh the pleasure of the disobedience" are "Lehmanisms" that have now become "McMorrisisms."

This book isn't full of common-sense parenting, because biblical parenting is neither common nor natural. It demands supernatural wisdom and power.

I commend to you John Lehman. It has been my great privilege to have him as a grad school professor, fellow pastor, running buddy, mentor, and friend. He is writing to you as a blessed success. His family of four children and three grandchildren is a living example of the faithfulness of God to a family that seeks to put Him first and keep His commandments.

So, read your Bible, read this book, and "serve the Lord with gladness!"

Jeremy McMorris,

Lead Pastor, Liberty Baptist Church, Dalhart, Texas

Acknowledgements

Special thanks to the following folks:

Ben and Candice Fetterolf, Seth and Cassie Martin, Cody Lehman, Sarah Porch, Gabriel Zarate, Caitlyn Lehman—your first reading and helpful comments were a great source of encouragement and direction.

Seth Martin—thanks for beginning the process of evaluating and assessing what was necessary to be consistent in my writing style.

Craig Seelig—thanks for the idea of " ... now what?" as well as helping me make sure my punctuation was appropriate.

Digby James—thanks for typesetting this and helping the presentation be so easily readable

Jim Holmes—thanks for helping me "get this book out of me!" Your attention to detail and expertise helped more than words can express.

Suzie Lehman—your consistent encouragement was such a resource of enablement and motivation.

Dedication

I would like to dedicate this book to Candice, Cassie, Cody, and Caitlyn, the children whom I have been privileged to rear in the nurture and admonition of the Lord, and to Suzie, my wife, with whom "my heart doth safely trust" (Proverbs 31:1, KJV). I also have been blessed to have two sons-in-law who have godly principles with which they desire to live their lives and invest in their own children.

This book was written as a follow-up to a request from our eldest daughters wanting some guidance in their consideration of, one day, being parents. My wife and I may not have always had the perfect methods in child-rearing, but we always had the right motives. We desired, above anything else, that you, our children, would love God with all your heart and would be willing to serve Him joyfully with your lives as you grew into adults.

One important part of your adult lives will be that of having and rearing children. With your exemplary lives, you have put credence to what I have taught in my role as a pastor. I thank you for your willingness to submit your own wills and to desire to serve Christ by obeying your parents. To be able to state publicly, in my ministry, the importance of abiding by standards and following through with discipline, and then to have you show that by being willing to do what was asked of you, has been a wonderful privilege. I now trust this book will be of assistance to you as you rear your own children.

I also trust the book will be of help to many other parents who will one day stand before God for the manner in which they disciplined and reared their children. Using God's Word as the premise has been my goal. God has promised to give wisdom liberally to each of us when we ask of Him. His Word is the primary source of this wealth of wisdom and must be our standard for parenting our children.

May God bless you all as you choose to follow Christ, submitting to Him as the standard for your own life and for the lives whom you will influence as parents. May God grant you the ability to do what you know should be done for His honor and glory.

A Note to the Reader

When mentioning children as individuals, reference may sometimes be made interchangeably between "he" and "she" in the pages that follow.

Preface

" **A** is for Adam, and in Adam's fall, we sinned all." So read the words of the magisterial New England Primer, first published between 1687 and 1690, used so effectively and extensively by the American nation's early settlers in the days of the founding fathers.

Because of the Fall—the historic event at the beginning of human history—sin has entered the world. And when it entered, it was guaranteed to be passed on to every child to be born in the human race.

Now you are a parent, you are the father or the mother of another sinner; maybe a beautiful and cute sinner, but a sinner nevertheless. And as you are a parent, a wonderful responsibility, yet a heavy one, rests upon you: as an instrument in the hands of God, you are to do your best to bring the life-transforming message of the Word of God—the gospel of His grace—to the little one entrusted to you. You are to do your best to bring that baby—that child—that adolescent—that young person—from the state of nature to a state of grace. "God ... now ... commands all people everywhere to repent" (Acts 17:30).

This little book will encourage you and direct you along the way to do your very best in this great task of parenting!

A glimpse into this chapter . . .

With electronic video devices or iPods, there are very specific, point-by-point instructions. Those are pieces of electronic equipment that one might keep for five years. During the process of child-rearing, although there is no training manual, you will be parenting your children daily for two decades! What's more, your parenting will influence your children for life!

... The goal is to have their children desire, above all else, to serve and please God with their lives.

"If any of you lacks wisdom, let him ask God, who gives generously to all without reproach, and it will be given him." (James 1:5).

Now what ... do we do to begin?

Getting ready to become a mom or dad

"It's Apparent ... We're Having a Baby!" Those are exciting words. Parents, whether biological or adoptive, are excited about the newness of life God gives through birth. The reality of all the responsibilities and requirements often does not set in until after the initial thrill of the baby's arrival. Then comes the realization that someone has to raise this child. That "someone" is the one who endured morning sickness and a variety of adjustments pregnancy brings prior to delivery. Or, in the case of an adoption, the ones who endured hours of paperwork, meetings, and great financial sacrifice to bring that child into their lives.

Consider the scenario for most young couples. They are blessed and excited about bringing their infant home from the hospital. Prior to leaving the hospital, they are given many instructions about insurance and other pertinent details. Once they arrive home and lay their infant in bed, it is very likely they will wonder, "Now what?" Parenting involves everything from changing a baby's diapers to correcting and directing a baby's strong will. Both require extreme patience and gentleness.

With electronic video devices or iPods, there are very specific, point-by-point instructions. Those are pieces of electronic equipment that one might keep for five years. During the process of child-rearing, although there is no training manual, you will be parenting your children daily for two decades! What's more, your parenting will influence your children for life! Not only are they influenced for life, but they will influence many others for a long time to come. There are many books and articles written about parenting, so, much of this has been written by someone else in a different way. I'm simply privileged to have been entrusted by God to rear four children and, through God's goodness and those experiences, I bring to you what has helped our family.

Qualifications of a Parent

It is incredibly important to evaluate why you should be a parent. Two questions come to mind that each parent needs to answer. The first is: "What qualifies you to *be* a parent?" This boils down to the biological result of a man and woman following God's plan for the procreation of children. God has commanded people to "replenish the earth" and, therefore, He has so orchestrated marriage to fulfill the desires and opportunity for procreation. Any married man or woman may be able to fulfill God's intended role for a parent. However, if the order of God's creation is violated by having a child out of wedlock, the parenting process is not negated. In whatever circumstance that child is placed, it is imperative that the child be reared in the nurture and admonition of the Lord (see Ephesians 6:4). This may necessitate the child being put up for adoption. Although it is difficult to put a newborn into another home, such an action applies the important principle of intentional parenting being the goal—rather than how the child came into the world.

However, just because you *can* be a parent doesn't always mean you are qualified appropriately. So, the next important question is: "What qualifies you *to parent*?" It is going to be extremely difficult to rear a child even under the most ideal circumstances—much more when life's often less-than-ideal events occur. Only the following of Scriptural principles can truly make someone qualified *to parent*.

Parents: Get Your Hearts Prepared.

"If any of you lacks wisdom, let him ask God, who gives generously to all without reproach, and it will be given him." (James 1:5). There will be many times when it will be difficult to know what is best to do. Those times of weakness will direct you promptly to ask God for His wisdom and help.

Prior to even knowing what topics are essential in the child-rearing process, it is vitally important that the committed couple specifically and intentionally get to know each other's strengths and weaknesses. Attraction to similar interests and special appeals will be the initial draw, and in order to succeed in their goals as time continues, the couple must become dedicated to working through difficulties together. Couples should not expect ease of parenting as a norm. Instead, they must strive together to request God's wisdom (that is—they should "ask God") and follow through with a common goal. Showing true commitment and kindness to your wife or husband reveals to your children your commitment and love to one who is still imperfect, but is content in the love that is provided.

Parents should be sure their personal relationship is what it is supposed to be—close fellowship with God. For parents to keep this in perspective, they need to inspect their desires to see that they align with God's own heart. They must "... seek first the kingdom of God and his righteousness, and all these things will be added to [them]" (Matthew 6:33). They also need to put into practice Psalm 37:4: "Delight yourself in the LORD, and he will give you the desires of your heart." (Psalm 37:4) If parents will seek to do what God expects from the very beginning, it will continue to be their focus. When they deviate from this, they must willingly seek His forgiveness, and the forgiveness of others, for the failure and resolve again to do that which is right.

The Goal of Parenting

God entrusts children to parents to be raised as lovers of God and followers of His Word. ("Train up a child in the way he should go; even when he is old he will not depart from it"—see Proverbs 22:6.) That means that to pass on the parents' interests, personalities, and talents is not the ultimate goal in child-rearing. The goal is to have their children desire, above all else, to serve and please God with their lives. God expects all parents to help their children become more adept in their natural skills and interests rather than to become clones of their parents. God would have every child realize that He, God, is supreme. When this occurs, the natural outcome will be that they will desire to be faithful children of God, loving and serving Him wholeheartedly.

Parenting requires wholehearted dedication to the task. Consider the following milestones, and endeavor to align them in the pattern of your parenting.

1. Understand the purpose of your child-rearing.

2. Discuss with your spouse any preconditioned expectations you may have.

3. Agree on a plan based on Scripture.

All young couples need to consider why they would and should have children. As was considered earlier, it is important to replenish the world according to God's good design. Going beyond that, parenthood is a way of producing disciples to fill the earth with God-worshippers. Parents need to empower their children to become mature and release them to become independent from them and dependent upon God.

The goal of this book is to help crystallize in parents' minds the importance of making the right choices for their children, and, through considering biblical principles that are laid out in God's Word, to please the Lord by the choices that are made and implanted. The goal in parenting comes to a final conclusion when their child reaches heaven. Until then, the pursuit of proper parenting must continue! For proper parenting to occur, God's Word must be used as the final authority on decisions and directions for parenting.

Adjusting Expectations

When one enters the novel world of parenthood, it will undoubtedly be with some expectations. These may come from a variety of experiences: how each parent was raised, how each parent wished he or she had been raised, how others were raised, and how God desires children to be raised. There will be many preconceived ideas that couples will bring into rearing their children. These ideas will come from their initial experiences as a child. Whether they have had good experiences or bad ones, these have helped formulate how they themselves will exercise their responsibilities as parents. There will be two different styles of rearing children brought into the marriage—one by each spouse. These experiences need to be discussed so that the couple can make the important decision to fulfill their role as parents as they believe God would have them, rather than based on how their parents raised them. The critical thing is not necessarily to glean all of the information and pool other people's experiences and then base the upbringing upon the popular vote. God wants parents to search the Scriptures and ask *Him* when they "lack wisdom."

In this light, it is extremely important that husband and wife in union consider all of their experiences, aligning their expectations with scriptural principles. As parents do this, their expectations will assist them in keeping their own opinions and experiences from ruling their thoughts. Instead, their focus will be on pleasing Christ.

A glimpse into this chapter . . .

A supreme goal to give your family is that they are to "serve the LORD with gladness." Anything and everything they do is to be with the joy of the Lord in their lives. As they observe mom and dad doing this, and are reminded when they as children are not, this will become a pattern that will be consistent for life.

Now what... do I want my child to be like when he grows up?

Preparing an overarching goal for your child

Ready, Steady ... Aim!

Now, what single motto would you instill in your child if you could boil everything down into one phrase? All children should desire, for their entire life, to serve the Lord with gladness! God desires all people to love Him. The way in which we show love to Him is by obeying Him. It's one thing to serve dutifully and upon demand with no enjoyment or purpose; it's altogether different to obey and serve with a purpose and goal. God allows His children individually to be able to be purposeful in everything they do. Serving with frustration, or as a terribly difficult task, can accomplish the goal of getting something done. However, it is so much more enjoyable to those who observe, as well as to the individual, to joyfully do what is requested. No one likes to have to demand something to be done and to have a bad attitude about it while it is taking place. The bad attitude is difficult for the one who made the requirement because he feels badly that the individual isn't enjoying what was asked. It is also difficult on the one who is frustrated at the task before him. Serving God with one's whole heart brings not only joy to Him, but to the ones who note the service, and especially to the one serving!

A supreme goal to give your family is that they are to "serve the LORD with gladness" (Psalm 100:2). Anything and everything they do is to be with the joy of the Lord in their lives. As they observe mom and dad doing this, and are reminded when they as children are not, this will become a pattern that will be consistent for life.

It is extremely important that parents decide on their own

expectations for child-rearing. One may initially think it is exciting to have children, and having seen other families, to want the enjoyment of family traditions and gatherings. However, once that child has entered the world, there is much training that will be required. To rear a child to serve and please God will require introducing and reinforcing with him biblical principles of what God expects. Consider what you want your child to be known for, and then pursue that with all your heart. In Proverbs 13:19, Solomon states how important it is to set proper expectations, for, "a desire fulfilled is sweet to the soul."

Samuel is a great example of a child who was dedicated to the Lord and who learned important truths, even if he wasn't always properly influenced by righteous people. The initial dedication to the Lord was what was so special about Samuel's life. Parents will not always have the perfect solution to parenting. If they will first and foremost determine early on that they want their child to grow up in the nurture and admonition of the Lord and will desire above all else to rear their young one "in the way he should go" (see Proverbs 22:6), then they will be on the right track to helping that child to be all that he or she should be. The human element in parenting will always be somewhat of an obstacle. God will intervene and bless in the child-rearing process, in and through the parent, as well as in spite of the parent, to help the child be what he or she is supposed to be.

Practical Wisdom from God's Word

Consider the following Scriptures as topics of training and do all you can to bring your child up in these areas:

> *Ask, and it will be given to you; seek, and you will find; knock, and it will be opened to you. (Matthew 7:7)*

It is wise to make sure children are eager to know what God expects of them. God desires that we ask of Him, seek Him, and implore Him in prayer. God will answer. We must always remember, though, that His answer may not always be what we want. A "no" from God is still an answer. A delay is still an answer. It is therefore important to be sure that children are taught to ask in such a way that they are seeking God's will to be done. Therefore, whenever an answer comes through that does not please us, if it is what God provides, then that is what He is most pleased with, and that makes it acceptable. Parents need to instill this by patterning it in their life as well. They need to be willing followers of what God does in and through the circumstances of life, rather than being frustrated when events don't go their way.

> *Be angry and do not sin; do not let the sun go down on your anger. (Ephesians 4:26)*

God knew that, because of our emotional makeup and selfish nature, we would get angry. One great means to keeping anger from controlling us is to keep short accounts. That's why, in

Scripture, people are taught to be sure that the sun did not set before they had sought forgiveness for wrongdoing. When someone stays angry, the spiral into bitterness begins and is so difficult to break. Also, when one remains angry, that person will continue to live by the flesh rather than revealing the fruit of the Spirit. No child should be allowed to stay angry, but if children see parents who hold grudges and are not harmoniously related to each other, they will very easily fall into the same actions. Therefore, it is important that parents not only teach this principle but also reveal it in their relationships with their spouses as well as with their children.

> *Be kind to one another, tenderhearted, forgiving one another, as God in Christ forgave you. (Ephesians 4:32)*

This verse reveals two important principles which must be implemented into a child's life: being kind and being forgiving.

Be kind. Although everyone seems to understand what kindness is, it seems easiest to spot when it is personally either received or not received. Unfortunately, people are not as concerned about whether they extend kindness or not. Kindness is a compilation of the many opportunities to put others before self. For one to be kind, that person must follow the example of Christ. It will be important to impress upon children that they must show kindness like Christ did. As Christ said:

> Give to everyone who begs from you, and from one who takes away your goods do not demand them back. And as you wish that

others would do to you, do so to them. "If you love those who love you, what benefit is that to you? For even sinners love those who love them. And if you do good to those who do good to you, what benefit is that to you? For even sinners do the same. And if you lend to those from whom you expect to receive, what credit is that to you? Even sinners lend to sinners, to get back the same amount. But love your enemies, and do good, and lend, expecting nothing in return, and your reward will be great, and you will be sons of the Most High, for he is kind to the ungrateful and the evil. Be merciful, even as your Father is merciful. (Luke 6:30–36)

It is easy to direct people to be kind, but not so easy to reveal it on your own. It takes completely submitting to God and His Word to sincerely be kind. Just like children learn how to verbalize, "I love you," because they hear it from the time they are babies and eventually mimic what they have been hearing, so, too, will they initially be kind if they are seeing and sensing kindness, both to themselves and, even more importantly, between their parents. So much is "caught" rather than "taught" in this issue.

To be kind, you must put on the example of Christ. Kindness is a compilation of the many opportunities to put others before self. It ties in nicely with esteeming others but makes it important in the manner of being kind enough to forgive and seek reconciliation. This must be exemplified, like so many other attributes, by the parent. It is easy to direct folks to be kind, but not so easy to reveal kindness on your own. It takes completely submitting to God and His Word to sincerely be kind.

Be forgiving. True biblical forgiveness is a must for families if they are to remain in a humble and Christlike attitude. Too often people may think that "to forgive" means "to forgive and forget." However, God has made us too smart to be able to forget. Rather, He has given us the perfect example of how forgiveness is to be extended. God Himself, when He forgives, removes our sins as far as the east is from the west (Psalm 103:12). This reveals that to truly forgive means that one does not bring up the sin again. It also reveals that the only reason to confront someone with a sin is when one is ready to forgive and restore. If one isn't willing to forgive, then the offense should not be brought up or it will simply heighten the already tense situation that folks are in when they are unforgiving. This must be first and foremost exemplified by parents as they forgive each other and as they choose not to bring up offenses again. Secondly, parents must forgive their children and never bring up offenses that have already been forgiven. Showing Christlike forgiveness is vitally important in teaching Christlike forgiveness.

Ask for forgiveness. All parents make mistakes, and the biggest mistake parents make is not thinking or admitting to this fact! One of the greatest weaknesses parents can have is that of failing to reveal Christlike conviction and a desire to reconcile. The first time a parent makes a mistake, he or she should eagerly and willingly admit the failure and say, "I am sorry. I was wrong; will you forgive me?" This reconciliation occurs so much more easily if it has been a practice and lifestyle commitment all through the married years. In His Word, God claims that it is *"good and pleasant"* when people—families— live together in unity (Psalm 133:1).

There will be times, though, that a couple has not practiced true and biblical conflict-management and resolution. When a family is not properly practicing the extension of forgiveness, it is kept from consistently being guilt-free. Christ encourages people to seek forgiveness so that restoration may be accomplished. Proper parenting continues when parents aren't provoking their children through a severed relationship.

So what's the *right* way to teach forgiveness? As a child sins or disappoints a parent, correction is very appropriate. Once that correction has been accomplished, the parent should be sure to have the child work through the biblical path of forgiveness. Admitting that one is wrong must be effected. In owning the act, an additional statement should be made that the child was wrong for doing the act. Finally, the child should verbalize, "I am sorry," and, "Will you forgive me?" By stating this and directly asking for forgiveness, the responsibility is then placed on the offended party to consider what was done, both in the wrong and in the desire to correct. The offended person or people then can grant the forgiveness needed in the repair of such a relationship. Once forgiveness has been granted, the past offense should not be brought up again. That is when the truth of biblical forgiveness will be realized.

It is critical that children be taught forgiveness as well as to see it properly practiced.

You shall be holy, for I am holy. (1 Peter 1:16b)

Everything that Christ did during His earthly ministry was done perfectly. He was able to patiently rebuke wrong and consistently love His enemies. He added credence to His message and ministry as One who was able to not only speak truth, but do so lovingly. Therefore, it is extremely important that anything and everything that is done as a parent is done with Christ as the pattern. If one would only consider how Christ would act and react and consistently follow that pattern, parents wouldn't provoke and offend their children or their spouses.

A person is known by how he responds and acts—not by what he says. Having character that is God-honoring requires always submitting to God. Exemplary character must be patterned after the principles of God's Word. One needs to have a foundational truth, God's Word, in order to understand and pattern a life after His. God's character is holy and just, and He commands us to be holy as He is. That doesn't mean we'll always attain that, but we should strive to pattern ourselves after His holiness. The pursuit of this kind of character will help people evaluate what God expects and then seek to fulfill His commands.

Blessed are those who hunger and thirst for righteousness. (Matthew 5:6)

Children must be taught that they are to seek to do all they can for God's glory. One great way to keep on that pursuit is to initially desire God's truth and way. When parents desire God, they will desire what God desires. Therefore, as they model this before their children, they will demonstrate how to pursue righteousness wholeheartedly.

Because of the frailness of sinners, it will always be a struggle to want what God wants, but if that's the initial desire, it will result in a very intentional pursuit of godly living.

Blessed are the meek. (Matthew 5:5)

Biblical meekness is "power under control." To have self-control is not easily taught, because it is so difficult to model. Everyone has his or her own talent and personality, views and opinions, and when these are willingly brought under submission to God's direction, it will be a wonderful example of bringing one's own desires and purposes under submission to what God would most desire. Parents must do this by exercising self-control in their various means of child-rearing.

Blessed are the poor in spirit. (Matthew 5:3)

Biblical humility implies that we see ourselves as God sees us: guilty. In regard to our own life and ability, we have nothing to be proud of. We are helpless sinners, guilty before God, and completely dependent upon His grace and mercy for deliverance.

Blessed are those who mourn. (Matthew 5:4)

Biblical mourning is the condition of being sorrowful for sin. Children need to see themselves as God does, and since " for all have sinned and fall short of the glory of God" (Romans 3:23), there is need of a Savior for their reconciliation. Teaching a child that he is a sinner, and that he must be sorry for and repent of those sins, will bring about the ultimate comfort he will ever receive: God's forgiveness.

Blessed are the merciful. (Matthew 5:7)

To give someone mercy, forgiveness, and kindness, when it is least deserved, is Christlike. Parents need to exercise this grace of mercy with each other as well as with their children. Mercy doesn't mean excluding right or overlooking wrong. When there is not a biblically-defined truth being violated, showing Christ's mercy will go a long way to assist a child's overall behavior.

Blessed are the pure in heart. (Matthew 5:8)

A person's true self will always be revealed. Christ tells us in Luke 6:45 that "out of the abundance of the heart his mouth speaks." So, the only way to have a pure life, one which pleases God and others, is to have a pure heart. This is generally found in the man or woman who always tries to see the best in others. Christ does not overlook sin, but continually loves the sinner. It is easy for parents or children to dislike and reveal disrespect and contempt for someone who acts differently than they do. Parents need to instill in their children a heart that accepts and appreciates someone even when that person is different. It is not a natural thing for a child to respect someone different or to respect and value people who are different because of sinful lifestyles or people who are different because of the way they exercise their Christian liberty. Yet, one with a pure heart—one which sees others as Christ does—will endeavor to love as Christ loves. One major way for this to be revealed is for parents to show their children love and kindness, even when they have been disappointed and sinned against.

> *Blessed are you when others revile you and persecute you and utter all kinds of evil against you falsely on my account. (Matthew 5:11)*

Unfortunately, righteous living does not always bring appreciation. Others will often disapprove or question motives when we are simply living like Christ. The best way to counter this, rather than feeling hurt and offended, is to thank God that being misunderstood or scoffed at is a credit to godly living. Be willing as parents to model this by being kind to those who may have caused personal offense. You can show this kindness by praying for them in front of your family and showing hospitality to them in your home.

> *Children, obey your parents in the Lord, for this is right. (Ephesians 6:1)*

There are always going to be specific areas where parents expect their children to obey. It begins with the essential understanding that they must obey, and that obedience is actually as if they were obeying the Lord. At times, it can become tedious to obey— even frustrating. Parents are not always going to be right and may even be a cause of frustration to their children at times. When the child doesn't feel like obeying, or when a parent isn't deserving of being obeyed, humanly speaking, as long as the child realizes that he or she is to obey as if obeying God, obedience will be the outcome. That type of obedience is a great resource. One of the greatest ways a child learns this lesson is by seeing how his parents honor God in their own lives.

Another key to help a child learn this lesson is when he or she watches the parents obey their human authorities—whether the law of the land or the requirements of their immediate bosses or supervisors in the workplace.

Finally, how mom submits to dad goes a long way in influencing how a child will submit to his or her parents.

[Children,] honor your father and mother. (Ephesians 6:2)

The actual act of obedience is not all that God expects of a child. There is to be honor that accompanies the act of obedience. The honoring will not only please God, but it will also make the obedience so much sweeter. It is easier to obey when one knows God is observing, and it is also easier to obey when one has the right attitude toward authority. An improper attitude feeds on rebellion, and rebellion continues the disobedience cycle. When children realize that honoring their parents pleases God, and when those children routinely demonstrate obedience as unto the Lord, they will want not only to obey, but also to honor as they ought for God's glory. There is a similarity in the way children observe their parents exercising obedience to authority, and how they observe their parents honoring each other.

A mom and dad who have mutual respect for each other, as with the exhortation in Ephesians 5 to submit to one another, will wonderfully reveal how the matter of honoring is to take place. Another element of vital importance is for children to see how their parents care for—and are kind to—their own parents. This truth is for life, yet it can be dangerously easy for parents to expect their own children to honor them without giving any thought to how they are honoring their own parents.

> *Delight yourself in the LORD, and he will give you the desires of your heart. (Psalm 37:4)*

All people know what they desire. The most important action, though, is what God desires. Therefore, the formula for doing what God desires is to delight in Him. This occurs initially by reading His Word. When a person delights in a certain event or topic, he or she spends a lot of time dwelling on and participating in it. After reading God's Word, obedience has to occur. An external display of merely reading the Bible is no sure mark of godliness.

For example, following God's precious Word reveals how important His truths are. Faithful church attendance reveals the value placed upon God's command of "not neglecting to meet together" in public worship (Hebrews 10:25). Having godly influence will help in godly pursuits. Finally, accepting and acting upon the conviction of the Holy Spirit reveals the importance one places upon His direction. As people delight in God, they are then allowed to pursue their interests, yet all the time desiring to please God in their pursuits. And, as they are willing to delight in God, if and when God changes their interests, they will still be privileged to enjoy their desires, for they are now operating within God's parameters.

> *Whatever you do, work heartily, as for the Lord and not for men.*
> *(Colossians 3:23)*

It is easy to work hard at what we are good at or in areas of our personal interests. However, God wants us to be just as interested in doing the difficult and unpleasant things with the same fervency and zeal. When a task is too difficult, or a circumstance isn't pleasing, using the biblical principle of doing the task as if God were observing and evaluating makes a tremendous difference. This will keep one focused on pleasing God rather than pleasing oneself or others.

The actual parenting chores are a great platform to exemplify this. When parents lovingly and joyfully serve their child, it will speak volumes as to how that child is treasured. It will also show that child how he or she is being given the same emotional and physical investment as something else the parents enjoy doing. If Christ came to earth to serve, then parents should not just teach their child how important it is to serve, but should consistently demonstrate how to do this.

Consistency in this area will be a wonderful exercise on the parents' part and a wonderful lesson learned by the child.

Do nothing from selfish ambition or conceit, but in humility count others more significant than yourselves. (Philippians 2:3)

Not only does God say we are to love others as we love ourselves, but He wants us to go one step beyond that. He desires that we treat others better than ourselves! That means we are to have a greater appreciation for another person's opinion than our own.

This can be revealed on a daily basis as parents reveal their desire to please each other above their own personal interests. This can also be exemplified to your child when he or she has a preference. If there is no biblical fault in what is desired or requested, then such preferences and requests ought to be taken into consideration *above* your own. This is very different from giving in and spoiling a child. It simply has to do with having your marital and parenting relationships governed by considering your spouse and your children more significant than yourself.

A man that hath friends must shew himself friendly. (Proverbs 18:24, KJV)

Everyone loves to be loved, but many people don't initiate that love. When people wait to be loved, they don't receive it. God wants all people to esteem others better than themselves (see

Philippians 2:3), so parents need to teach their children how to proactively look out for the interests of others. Selfishness looks inward while unselfishness looks outward. To truly help children do this will initially require that mom and dad are looking out for each other's interests. They should work the hardest at asking how they can serve rather than be served. It is so easy to wait to be served and not initiate the service.

Parents can model this in an even greater way as they endeavor to serve their children. They don't need to wait for "thanks" (although that principle will be addressed) for them to serve. Christ served because of our need, not because we deserved or appreciated His help. Therefore, with that example, it is important to remember that Christ came not to be served, but to serve (Mark 10:45).

Children need to see parents reaching out to folks who need friends, and asking the ones needing help into their homes rather than simply gravitating toward those who are the more affluent and influential. Parents should ask people into their home who will more than likely never reciprocate—that is the idea of showing oneself friendly (see Luke 14:12–14). Just asking the question, "What would Jesus do?" can remind us to be friendly and loving. God loves a cheerful giver, and one of the least expensive gifts we can give—in monetary terms— is our friendship. Allowing our lives to reach out and touch the lives of other people will go a long way in showing them Christ. Honor God by being, like him, "a friend of ... sinners" (Matthew 11:19).

Give thanks in all circumstances; for this is the will of God in Christ Jesus for you. (1 Thessalonians 5:18)

It is easy to be thankful when circumstances are positive! It's very difficult to have that same attitude when life seems treacherous or unfair. When a child has been trained and believes that God does all things well and that He sees the "big picture," then that child can trust Him that "all things work together for good, for those who are called according to his purpose" (Romans 8:28). This trust will encourage thanksgiving even in the hardest times because the ultimate good is not present pleasure but eternal purpose. Therefore, children need to be thankful for whatever circumstances or materials they receive. Giving thanks is in God's will. As children continue to give thanks, they will also continue on the path of learning to follow God's will in many other circumstances as well.

Judge not, that you be not judged. (Matthew 7:1)

Children need to be sure they are not judging others based on their own preferences or pursuits. They should evaluate other people based on how God would evaluate them, and accept them that way. If God would love, then they need to do the same. Parents can show their children how to give generous interpretations—that is, giving the benefit of the doubt. It can be both "taught" and "caught" through what the parents do and say. This will be greatly exemplified if parents do not jump to conclusions but are certain of their evaluations. Considering others better than oneself will help establish a positive evaluation of others, even when they disagree with what has been said or when you disagree with how they do something. This gives your children an example of extending to others the same liberty that you personally desire.

> *Do not lay up for yourselves treasures on earth, where moth and rust destroy and where thieves break in and steal, but lay up for yourselves treasures in heaven, where neither moth nor rust destroys and where thieves do not break in and steal. (Matthew 6:19–20)*

Treasures are items and symbols which, in our view, hold value. True treasure is what God would have us appreciate. Having a nice item is acceptable as long as that is not what brings ultimate satisfaction. One should be willing to give up something of earthly value to gain what is of heavenly worth. This principle will not be instilled in a child unless that child sees his or her role models give up what is observed as valuable on earth because it will bring glory to God for eternity.

> *... let your light shine before others, so that they may see your good works and give glory to your Father who is in heaven. (Matthew 5:16)*

It is not easy to live for Christ. When others encounter a Christlike lifestyle, it is possible that those following Christ will be mocked. We must realize that a glimpse of Christ in our lives requires our being completely sold out to Him. Parents need to model

Christlikeness to each other and to their neighbors and acquaintances so that their children can see that living for God is not only done within the church walls or when they are in the presence of other Christians.

Practical examples can be set when, for instance, customer satisfaction does not go their way. That is the perfect test of being a "shining light" before others! It is so easy to "shine" when everything is pleasant. When things are not going satisfactorily, and parents can still smile and be pleasant, they are patterning this verse.

> *You shall love the Lord your God with all your heart and with all your soul and with all your strength and with all your mind, and your neighbor as yourself. (Luke 10:27)*

God desires that He have first place in our lives. Mom and dad, if you want your children to burn with the same passion, manifesting that God has first place in all things, you must live it out yourselves. Having the attitude that whatever God wants is what they personally want is vitally important.

Being content with fewer dollars and "toys," along with demonstrating a complete trust and appreciation for what God has done, reveals a supreme love for God. Everything in a parent's life should show the child that there is nothing more important than loving God supremely. As the child observes this, and is challenged himself to note and follow, it will help him want to follow God's Word in the same manner.

You shall ... love your neighbor as yourself. (Luke 10:27b)

We have an abundance of selfish love directed towards our personal lives and interests. A life that directs that love toward others will take a lot of effort but will be one that consistently reveals to your children that Christ's example of selfless service toward our neighbor is not just a thought, but a reality.

God uses the example of the Good Samaritan to display how we are to love a neighbor. The man who was in need of help was definitely a man in need and was not in any position to repay any of the kindness extended to him. It is quite easy to help someone who will return the favor, but to love someone—especially someone whom others don't love—reveals great love on your part. This love must be extended by mom and dad to each other first and foremost. When you, as a parent, put your spouse first before your own desires, your children get to see what it means to love your neighbor as yourself. It is also extremely important that mom and dad put the child's desires above their own.

Pray without ceasing. (1 Thessalonians 5:17)

An attitude of prayer is very important. When God says we are to continually pray, He desires our consistent communication with Him throughout the day. When we are willing to speak to the Lord, we are going to be aware of proper actions and attitudes throughout the day as well.

We can ask for help for routine situations—safety and

strength—while also requesting God's intervention in overcoming temptation. This will keep us from yielding to temptations the devil is always bombarding us with. When a child is taught to remain in an attitude of prayer, he will find grace to avoid many temptations and to sincerely ask God's rescue when temptation is unavoidable.

Do not quench the Spirit. (1 Thessalonians 5:19)

To resist or to "turn off" the powerful influences of the Holy Spirit (as one would turn off a faucet to stop the flow of water) is to go against a holy God. It is God's purpose to have the Holy Spirit constantly encouraging or convicting us to do what most pleases Him. When we are convicted by the Holy Spirit, it is in our best interest to listen and heed, for that will continually keep us doing what is right and refraining from evil. As God has said (see Revelation 3:20), He is at our heart's door wanting to come in and direct us, but, if we refuse that, we will keep ourselves from doing what is right. Children need to have this ever before them, realizing that, if and when they sin, they are not just hurting their parents or their own reputation, but they are hurting God.

Rejoice always. (1 Thessalonians 5:16)

We should realize that "always" means all the time! Parents need to remember that God is in control and all circumstances must be used to bring glory to Him! This needs to be taught and exemplified by parents.

If one is accustomed to rejoicing only in pleasurable circumstances—when receiving gifts, kind acts, etc—then when life isn't so giving or pleasurable, it will be difficult to rejoice. True happiness is not just rejoicing when "good" happens to us but rejoicing in the One who orchestrates what happens to us. If a child is taught that the rejoicing is in the fact that God is God and that He will do what is best and right for us, then, even if the child becomes sad because of a loss, he or she can be rejoicing in God who never changes!

> *But seek first the kingdom of God and his righteousness, and all these things will be added to you. (Matthew 6:33)*

God wants all people to desire Him more than they desire anything else this world has to offer. For this to take place effectively, it will require that parents are more interested in God's will than anything else. It is important to provide a living for your family and to have adequate provisions. However, it does not mean that people will overlook God to "get ahead" in this world. They will, instead, consider what God has purposed for them during this time. They should seek God first by wanting to please God before pleasing themselves and their family.

> *Let what you say be simply "Yes" or "No". (Matthew 5:37)*

Children need to know that words mean something. It is of particular importance that parents pattern this by being truthful themselves in what they say.

If you say you will do something tomorrow, then be sure you do so! Giving children false hope (because a parent merely wants to get them to wait or leave them alone) just teaches children to lie to get people to quit expecting something. Then, when that "something" doesn't occur, they can just simply say they forgot or that something else came up. That is lying! So, without having to say, "I promise" or, "really, honestly," parents are simply instructing children that when their "yes" is stated, they mean exactly what is stated, (meaning that whatever comes from their lips is truth) which will be a wonderful lesson in integrity.

All of the good intentions of parenting can very easily be lost if truth is not a foundational principle. If parents will follow through with statements made, and responses and promises to children are always fulfilled, then they will easily believe, and trust, their parents. But, when excusing (and, therefore, breaking) promises becomes a habit, then children can easily apply that to other areas of their speech.

... speaking the truth in love. (Ephesians 4:15)

"Words mean something." Tell the truth—always! Anything you say, back it up with follow through or explanation. It is so easy to make comments in an unthinking manner, whether it is because you are hoping that topic and circumstance will take place, or simply stated so that it is put off for later. It is extremely important for parents not to have idle words. You must be intentional in your words, otherwise your children will hear and understand something completely different than you intended.

Yet, as you speak the truth, speak it in love. Remember, although you are the parent, children are still to be considered better than yourself (see Philippians 2: 3. That doesn't mean that you don't have any authority over them. You may need to adjust your expectations, but your children are still to be treated with love. Just like God, you, as a parent, are to have the proper measure of justice and love directed at your children. You must love as Christ loves, and give of yourself. However, you are still to correct and direct as Christ would. You are to love them like God loved you, and therefore love them wholly, and so direct them accurately in the truth.

For whatever one sows, that will he also reap. (Galatians 6:7)

A consequence is often considered a negative word. However, according to God's Word, there are both negative and positive connotations to it. If one "sows sparingly [one] will also reap sparingly, and whoever sows bountifully will also reap bountifully." (2 Corinthians 9:6). The same holds true in rearing children. Investing time and energies, while consistently, lovingly, and patiently fulfilling parental duties, shows how obedience is sought.

A glimpse into this chapter . . .

Obedience is an essential ingredient for proper family order. If proper obedience is not instilled in children, all other efforts are useless. Obedience is simply following what is stated; it is a child doing what he is told to do. It seems so simple, but one little deviation from what is told can change both the authority's and follower's perspective of the situation.

Now what ... does obedience mean?

Demonstrating what it means to live in submission to the one, true God

Coming to the Obedience of the Faith

One of the greatest concerns of the apostles and early church leaders was to fulfill the words of Jesus in Matthew 28:18— to spread the message of His love and grace, making people His disciples or followers. A disciple is a learner, one who obediently follows his or her master. The Apostle Paul, in Romans 1:5 and 15:18, mentioned his concern to bring people to the obedience of the faith. Writing elsewhere to the Ephesians, he assumed that those converts were no longer the "sons of disobedience" (Ephesians 2:2, 5:6) but rather were being obedient to God in His call to them to become Christlike.

There is nothing more frustrating in the grocery store checkout line than watching an unruly child manipulate his mother. Why? Because to observe one so innocent, young, and helpless controlling the entire situation not only reveals the improper behavior of the child, but also reveals the lack of control that parent has. A person wouldn't become a horse owner if he didn't first of all have a plan for governing and controlling his horse. An unruly horse is worthless; it might as well remain wild on the range. An ungoverned, unruly child will become exactly that—worthless for God's glory.

Obedience is an essential ingredient for proper family order. If proper obedience is not instilled in children, all other efforts are useless. Obedience is simply following what is stated; it is a child doing what he is told to do. It seems so simple, but one little deviation from what is told can change both the authority's and follower's perspective of the situation.

Children will often reject or strongly oppose reasonable

instructions. When this occurs, it is critical at this point that they are taught to obey according to the true character of obedience. Obedience, in its truest form, is simply doing what you are told. To determine what you want from your child requires certain expectations. Because it is difficult to know exactly what is going to be expected of a child prior to its arrival, many specific details are not even considered.

God's Word: The Absolute Standard

Your own parents, other parents, and specific books will all have different opinions of what is important in the child-rearing process. What one person expects, another person may not have even considered. Therefore, it is important for you as the parents to pray and realize the responsibility of child-rearing will fall squarely on *your* shoulders.

You are not left without truth as your guide. You must base your expectations and discipline on the godly principles found in Scripture. Consider what principles a child should have instilled in his or her life and then begin that pursuit, whether before or after the child's birth. Remember, whatever is going to be expected must be inspected.

Ephesians 6:4 commands fathers—and by extension, parents—not to provoke their children to wrath. This is the idea of needlessly frustrating a child. This often happens when the rules and expectations keep changing. One parent may really want the child to use terms such as "Yes sir" or "No ma'am" when speaking, and another may simply require "Yes" or "No." There is nothing wrong with either expectation, and neither is intrinsically better or worse than the other. The frustration comes when the expectations are always changing. As parents, you must be in agreement on the expectations you hold for your child's behavior and then follow up on these expectations. Acknowledge and reward the proper behavior, and discipline the unacceptable behavior.

If a child brings a glass of water into a room that has been deemed off-limits for food and drink—and this detail is understood by the child—then the parent must discipline that action. When the parent overlooks the glass of water until it has been spilled, then any discipline will be out of anger and selfishness and will not model consistency.

Without these defined expectations, nothing will be accomplished. Proverbs 13:19 states that "a desire fulfilled is sweet to the soul." Goal-setting and implementation of a plan to reach those goals is central to the overall pattern of proper child-training.

Old Testament Examples

Two great examples of obedience are found in the Old Testament.

Saul: 1 Samuel 15:1–23 relates the story of Saul. Saul was told in the previous chapter to completely destroy the godless nation including all living things. A great victory was accomplished by Saul and the children of Israel, and all were killed except for one person and the healthy animals. When Samuel came to help in the offering of a sacrifice, he found Saul already preparing to offer the sacrifice himself. Samuel also noted additional noises in the background and confronted Saul about his initial command and his follow-through with that command. Unfortunately, Saul had kept the good animals along with King Agag.

The people of Saul's day would have marveled at how great a king Saul was because he not only conquered the people but kept the king as a kind of showpiece. Because of Saul's improper behavior, Samuel's response was that God would much rather have obedience than offerings or sacrifices. As a result of this circumstance, Saul actually lost his privilege of being king.

Abraham: Genesis 22 relates the story of Abraham and his willingness to obey God. God asked Abraham to take his only son to the mountain and offer him as a sacrifice. Abraham demonstrated his obedience by rising early the following morning to follow through with what he was told to do. Not only did he rise up early, but he also made every provision to follow through with what he was told to do by making sure he had the wood and the knife and the rope to make a proper sacrifice unto the Lord. It wasn't until Isaac was on the altar that God revealed an alternative for the sacrifice.

Obedience Is Essential!

As 1 Samuel 15:22–23 asks, "Has the Lord as great delight in burnt offerings and sacrifices, as in obeying the voice of the LORD? Behold, to obey is better than sacrifice, and to listen than the fat of rams. For rebellion is as the sin of divination ..." Satan would have everyone desire to be above God and to consider rebellion of spirit and tongue better than doing what God desires.

Always obey. As noted in this book, according to Ephesians

6:1, children are to obey their parents as they are to obey God. This rule is as hard on parents as it is on children. It requires the parents to be sure they are concerned with the follow-through of the rules they deemed so important from the beginning. Not only is obedience important to maintain order in a child's life, it also has profound spiritual implications. One of the most basic obligations a Christian has is to obey God.

Romans 6:16 states that the one to whom people submit and obey reveals whose servants they really are. God has stated in this passage that obedience actually leads one to righteousness. Another way to say this is that it reveals the righteous by their willingness to obey. Obeying God is always right. As children obey, they develop an even greater awareness of righteousness in their lives. Parents, by instilling this principle, will do their children a great spiritual favor.

The Qualities of True Obedience

Obedience is not simply doing something, after being warned and intimidated into the behavior. Obedience requires an immediate response, a complete response, a willing response, and an acceptable response. If one obeys after much fuming and fretting, that is still not obedience. If one obeys immediately but does not complete the task, then it is also not complete obedience. If one obeys immediately and even completely, but complains the entire time the task is being done, that is not obedience. If one challenges the authority of the parents while completing the task without violating any of the previous responses, this is still not obedience.

The biblical examples of Saul and Abraham reveal how important it is to fulfill every aspect of the obedience factor. In Saul's case, he actually obeyed in three of the four requirements. He not only immediately went to battle, but willingly and acceptably did so as well. His incomplete obedience was the fact that he did not *completely* obey. Because of that, God removed the kingdom from him.

However, in Abraham's case, he followed through in every capacity—even to the point of preparing to kill his son as an offering. Although Abraham had to wait until he was 100 years old to have a son, and he had been promised that his offspring would be as many as the sand of the sea and the stars of the sky, he still did not delay in his obedience to the command of offering his son as a sacrifice to God.

According to Genesis 22, after God had commanded Abraham to take his son and offer him as a burnt offering, Abraham revealed the manner in which all children (and adults, for that matter) should obey. He obeyed in the following manner:

Immediately—one must do right, right away. There should be no counting to three, repeatedly requesting, or only after the decibel level rises to the point the child knows there will be an eruption. "Decibel-level discipline" only reveals terror and fright and never requires an immediate response. Using the example of Abraham, a parent should emphasize how important it was to obey right away, as he obeyed "early" the next morning. There wasn't a delay in his desire to obey!

Completely—neither half-hearted nor partial obedience is acceptable. To clean a room, for example, is to make sure the closets and surfaces beneath the bed are just as clean as the parts that are easily observable. For a child to completely obey, he or she must do all that is asked without trying to get out of any portion of the assigned task. Abraham did exactly that. He actually made sure he had the knife and wood and did not leave anything at home to make the offering occur.

Willingly—this means the child must obey without complaint. Even if the child should eventually do the work or even if he begins following through right away but is defiant during his "obedience," that is still not proper. One must do what is right because it is the right thing to do, not because one agrees with or is in favor of the action. Abraham willingly prepared for the sacrifice because he desired to follow through in the exact manner in which God had commanded. He didn't ever complain or want more time but acted upon God's requirement.

Acceptably—this means the obedience must occur without challenge. Children are not to decide on their own whether it is appropriate for them to obey this rule. They are simply to do what is required, no matter how they feel or whether others are required to do the same. Whether something seems "fair" or not, children are still to do what is expected. Abraham again was the model for this, as he never once challenged God that he could never have many descendants if he killed this first one.

Fighting a Sin Nature

Because discipline takes such a concentrated measure of effort, and many other details can get in the way, people often would rather have someone else rear their child or allow her to choose her own way. This ultimately reveals the lack of discipline in the parents' lives. Although it appears the child is unruly and a frustration, it is really the parents' fault for allowing her to become that way. All children, because of Adam, as well as their parents, are sinful by birth and by choice. Sin, in its deepest root, is selfishness—wanting one's own way at the cost of God's glory and others' good. Therefore, when the child repeatedly wants her own way, she is only acting out her sin nature. Not until the parent systematically disciplines and requires obedience will the child note the necessity to change. Even then there will be a battle of wills.

Three Overriding Rules for Your Family—The Rest Hang on These!

Obey: There is no substitute for obeying. Simply stated, what is expected and stated by a parent must be followed by a child. God's Word highlights that children must obey their parents— it is commanded and expected by God. There is no substitute for obedience. No matter what the expectation, or understanding, obedience must occur.

No amount of rationalizing can override the term "obey." Simply stated, obeying is doing what one is asked by one's proper authority. God expects obedience, and if this is not a major emphasis, then nothing else in the parenting really matters. If children don't obey their parents, they won't obey God, and that runs contrary to all that God commands!

Speak the Truth: The important aspect of telling the truth is that Satan is the one who initiated lying, and when people lie, they are following the plan of the devil. Jeremiah 17:9 states that the "heart is deceitful above all things, and desperately sick; who can understand it?" Children are to be kept from developing a life pattern like Satan's, so this tendency must be stopped right away. The discipline is for the actual telling of the lie, not for any embarrassment this caused or any other issue promoted.

The whole family, including parents, are to speak the truth. Especially as children mature into adulthood, and then as they continue throughout life, parents must respect them and treat them with complete human dignity. Children, in turn, should respect their parents. Parents and children must be taught to respect all other humans.

Respect others: Satan is the primary example of one who rebelled. His rebellion was not respecting God in heaven. Jude 8 states that one of the elements of sin is when one would "reject authority, and blaspheme the glorious ones."

While obedience in the previous pattern is critical, it is also important that parents should not provoke their children.

Have an appeal process

One way to avoid provoking children is to institute an appeal process. This provides the child the opportunity (but only once per circumstance) to literally appeal the decision that the parents may have come to. This will allow a positive, open communication to take place between the parents and child but is not one that takes advantage of the situation or parent.

For an appeal process to function properly, and to avoid provoking their children to anger, parents should be sensitive to special situations and concerns children may have. In the appeal process, the child requests that the parent change his instructions or discipline based on new facts of which the parents were not previously aware of or that the child thought they did not understand. By training a child to appeal, parents can avoid conflict without compromising their authority.

Appeals must be made to the parent currently giving instructions or discipline. And, it is critical that the appeal is made to the parent involved in the situation, and not made to one who doesn't know the entire circumstance.

Appeals to parents will only be entertained when the child comes with a meek attitude. The "Why can't I?", "Do I have to?" and "But mom" attitude is not an appeal but a complaint or challenge to authority. Appeals should only be made once. Once the appeal has been made, whether the answer is to the child's favor or not, it is never to be repeated and the child has to accept "no" gracefully and do what has been decided. The appeal is only allowed when a major concern on the child's part has arisen because of an unknown piece of information. Children may use the phrase "May I appeal?" This acknowledges that the parent is in authority. The wording may be different than that, but there must not be a challenge of authority.

A glimpse into this chapter . . .

Different stages of a child's life allow for different disciplines. The discipline is not applied because of anger or embarrassment, but to reinforce the sense of wrongdoing and further the child's fulfillment of parental expectations. At no time is it right for a parent to discipline for any other reason than simply to instill the importance of there being inspection for expectations. The ultimate goal is not the initial "inspection," but the overall process of bringing the child to fulfill the goals that have been set early in the process of child-rearing.

Now what… do I do if my
child disobeys?

Facing the consequences God has directed
when there is disobedience

S tephen had been warned three times not to run up the stairs. His parents repeatedly instructed him that there was the danger that he could trip, fall and hurt himself badly, as well as possibly damage nearby artwork at the bottom of the stairs of their condo.

Stephen, however, was determined to manage the stairs in his own way, and at his fastest speed.

His parents were concerned that they did not wish him to obey their instruction merely as a form of grudging submission, but in a spirit of obedience from the heart. They knew that, important as achieving the outcome was (not running up the stairs and risking life and limb as well as incurring collateral damage!), it was also important for Stephen to appreciate that there was good reason for the fact that they required his consistent and unquestioning obedience.

It is right for you, as a parent, to expect obedience from your child. Obedience has to be from the heart. So, when there is a consistent lack of obedience, the heart must be reached, a process which may involve several stages or steps.

Parents must remember the important aspect of shepherding their child's heart during this entire process. It is not a burden to fulfill a responsibility given by God. As parents lead their children, realizing God has placed each one of them in their home for their specific discipleship, they will continually be challenged to do all they can for His glory.

It is one thing to have expectations, but they are only as good as the reinforcement they are given. For expectations to be effective, inspections—progress checks—must be made along the way. If the expectations are not fulfilled as stated, then a decision must be made. Either the expectation can be overlooked, or it can be reinforced. The most difficult part of a goal is not the setting of it, but the implementation of the goal. If the statements portray what parents want instilled in their child's life, and if they sincerely desire children to obey and honor, then there must be reinforcement, or discipline, for the misbehavior.

Different stages of a child's life allow for different disciplines. The discipline is not applied because of anger or embarrassment, but to reinforce the sense of wrongdoing and further the child's fulfillment of parental expectations. At no time is it right for a parent to discipline for any other reason than simply to instill the importance of there being inspection for expectations. The ultimate goal is not the initial "inspection," but the overall process of bringing the child to fulfill the goals that have been set early in the process of child-rearing.

God has definitely created a part of the body to receive spankings when they are necessary. The purpose of the spanking, as stated in His Word, encourages this so that the child will not bring his mother (or father) to shame and that the child, in turn, will be blessed. "The rod and reproof give wisdom, but a child left to himself brings shame to his mother." (Proverbs 29:15) The "rod and reproof" (terms for discipline and correction) are for the express purpose of helping the child become a vessel for God's glory. There should never be the attitude that the child is a burden to the parent because of the need to discipline. Rather, the motivation to discipline is so the child will be reminded to live according to godly expectations for him, which, in turn, pleases God, bringing Him glory, and bringing the child His blessing.

Wisdom from the Word of God

"Discipline your son, and he will give you rest; he will give delight to your heart" (Proverbs 29:17).

There is a peace and calm which parents experience when their children are obeying and following biblical principles in their lives. There will not be the constant nervousness or uncertainty which accompanies one who never knows if his child will obey.

"Folly is bound up in the heart of a child, but the rod of discipline drives it far from him" (Proverbs 22:15).

People are sinners by nature and by choice. From birth, children demonstrate this in no uncertain terms! Sin is inherent in all children, brought down through the ages and passed on by you, their parents. Because of this, sin needs to be corrected—in such a way that children will remove it from their lives. As they continue to mature, they will, undoubtedly, constantly be tempted to sin. This reveals the purpose of the discipline—a constant reminder that they need to remove this from their lives to be best used of the Lord.

"Do not withhold discipline from a child; if you strike him with a rod, he will not die" (Proverbs 23:13).

This is a clear reminder that the child is only being disciplined for his or her good and present and future service for God. It does get tiring disciplining a child, repeatedly having to be aware of the expectations initially set up, and then the continued inspections. However, with the goal of God-honoring obedience, you will continually realize how important it is to remain faithful to the task.

*   *   *

What are the legal considerations of spanking your child? This varies from state to state and country to country. As an example, the following quotation is from the Children's Law Center, School of Law, University of South Carolina:

Corporal punishment may be administered as a method of discipline provided that it is: a) administered by a parent or guardian; b) for the sole purpose of restraining or correcting the child; c) is reasonable in manner and moderate in degree; d) has not brought about permanent damage to the child; and e) is not reckless or grossly negligent.

This is a state licensing and, along with God's proven Word, reveals that it is also noted by the government as permissible.

Seven Matters for You to Establish

1. Establish ahead of time the basis for disciplining your children.

It is extremely important to remember the initial reason you have set up guidelines and expectations for a child. Parents who remember that their goal is to bring their child up in the nurture and admonition of the Lord will constantly evaluate and determine the progress and see if their child is obeying. There are not different levels of disobedience, in just the same way as there are not different levels of lying. A lie is a lie, and a disobedient act is disobedience. Every willful act of defiance and disobedience should be disciplined.

2. Establish ahead of time the standard implements for administering discipline.

God, in His Word, has stated that parents should use a "rod." This was actually a small sapling or branch, quite supple, and, if applied, would instill a sharp reminder to the child because of the slight pain applied. The striking of the child is not intended for pain so they hurt because of his or her wrongdoing, but as a reminder of wrongdoing. It is to bring him or her into the reality of the moment—that something has been done wrong, and since a verbal reminder hadn't been effective, or a previous reminder didn't affect the behavior, this would. The reminder is not for immediate pain and frustration, but to realize the purpose of the discipline—parental expectation for God-honoring obedience. Parents may choose to use a switch, paint stick, glue stick, paddle, belt, or similar item. The purpose for determining in advance what will be used is so, in the moment of application of the rod, they are not using their hand or just any other item that may be nearby.

3. Establish a standard place to administer discipline.

This allows the child and parent to know that the discipline is an intentional, goal-oriented process rather than just a reaction to displeasure. Having a set place for this will also allow for there to be a starting and stopping of the discipline. Parents may want to use the bathroom, hallway, parents' bedroom, etc. Wherever the discipline takes place is not an off-limits location for other interactions, but is a place where all parties know that correction, intentional and non- reactionary, will occur.

4. Establish standard discipline policies.

This assists parents from reacting improperly to the situation. There are times that some circumstances may be considered cute rather than wrong. If there is no set policy in place, when a certain act of disobedience occurs, the child might not even be disciplined. On the other hand, if the child's wrongdoing really embarrasses or infuriates the parent, then the parent might spank a lot more. The purpose for the policy is so that there is consistency.

One policy is how many swats you will give in your spanking. This should be the same for every willful disobedient act. The younger the child is, the less the force of the swat should be.

There is no such thing as a "paddleometer" but, if there were, you would judge the spanking on the intensity so the child recognizes the wrongdoing. Remember, the pain of the discipline must outweigh the pleasure received in the disobedience. If discipline does not affect the child enough to bring a realization that there is a negative consequence to such behavior, then he or she may consider that it's not worth obeying the next time. The intent of the discipline is so that the reminders of the past progressively instill discipline in the child so that he or she will not want to do wrong because it is wrong to do wrong.

Some examples are: if your child is resistant to being spanked, you will have it doubled, (perhaps you will spank five swats per offence), your child must stop crying in a reasonable time or that will be considered further disobedience. (The crying itself is not the wrong; it is the fact that once it has been determined that the child has done wrong, and discipline has taken place, the child will be responsible to exercise self-control rather than being mad and crying for attention or out of anger.) When parents determine the policies in advance, their reaction will be intentional rather than reactionary. It is always worth reminding a child that the spanking or discipline is not the choice of the parents; rather, it was the child's choice to do wrong, so the parents had to follow through. It may even add a little levity to tell your child, "You will either do this with a spanking, or without!" Either way, the child must obey and if he or she chooses to obey before the discipline, that's the desired goal and actually the preferred result, both for parents and child.

5. Establish the fact that you will always stay in control.

Always make it a point to realize that your goal is to bring God glory through the child's life. You are not concerned about whether or not you are embarrassed, frustrated, or anything else. You simply want to help your child become, and remain, God-honoring throughout his entire life. So, if you are angry, wait until you gain control before you discipline. If you discipline improperly with a wrong attitude or behavior, you will need to contend with your own sin issue while disciplining. This defeats the purpose of your parenting at that moment. You may need to put off the actual discipline for a short time until you gain control of yourself and come back to realize that your goal is to bring glory to God, not simply rest to yourself. If you have disciplined improperly, then seek forgiveness! When a child observes his parents seeking and extending biblical forgiveness, it reinforces the pattern and principle of the instruction.

6. Establish the fact that you will speak the truth in love to your children, whether during discipline or casual conversation.

Parents typically have the right motives in mind when it comes to rearing children in the nurture and admonition of the Lord, but, if not careful, they will use the wrong methods. Being impatient with children and revealing a frustration with their behavior will only encourage them to be provoked rather than to feel loved. Children are "adults in process" and should be treated with the dignity that adults expect to be treated. There is definitely a difference between a child and an adult when it comes to both ability and responsibility. However, it does not diminish the importance of treating them just like parents are teaching them to treat others. In fact, one of the best means in which children learn is to have examples before them. The ones most likely to mentor and disciple children are their parents. Parents will direct and lead them by their examples much more strongly than by their words. As the saying goes, "Your actions are so loud, I can't hear what you are saying."

Too often, parents wonder why and when their children stopped obeying. They believe they have "trained" them because they have "taught" them. Unfortunately, the "training" came when they lived improperly before their children, creating terrible examples of the principles they so desired to teach. Two examples come to mind:

When and if a mom is not submissive and obedient to her husband, she will give direct contradiction to the fact that children should obey;

When and if a dad is not submissive and obedient to the Lord, he will demonstrate the same contradiction.

Parents need to realize their actions, in these incidents, are observed and followed, either positively when parents obey

God's Word completely, or, negatively, when parents are not obeying. Parents should strive to live holy and humble lives, seeking to be holy, yet recognizing when they are not, and living out repentance to God and to those who are wronged.

7. Establish reconciliation procedures.

Following every disciplinary encounter, there should be closure. One of the greatest results of discipline is that the incident is completed. A child should not be told he is so bad and he needs to do right, and then not be given the chance to have the sin duly addressed by discipline, and then have the sin forgiven.

By telling your children they are wrong, and then disciplining them and offering complete reconciliation, you show the process was undertaken in love and care rather than in frustration and anger. All parents ought to make sure their children know they love them, both prior to the actual disciplinary procedure, as well as following. A great way to make sure there is complete understanding is to explain why they are having the discipline prior to the discipline. They should know that an expectation for God's glory was violated. As a result, to follow through with the commitment to "bring [children] up in the discipline and instruction of the Lord," (Ephesians 6:4), this discipline must be implemented. Following this, though, parents should hug the child and say, "I love you," and even have a conversation—providing a reminder that you only spank if there is disobedience, so that is the reason you are following through. You still love your child as always.

A glimpse into this chapter . . .

Consider the whole matter of responsibility, and how to cultivate it. Life is not made up of coasting through easy or enjoyable tasks. No wonder snooze buttons are placed on alarm clocks and people are given "grace" periods—people don't initially like to do things exactly when they are to do so. There is nothing wrong with not liking a given responsibility, but there is a lot wrong with not following through with what must be done.

God clearly states that parents are to be living examples before their children. According to Deuteronomy 6:6–7, parents are to be directing their children to love God with their lives as well as their words. Parents are to constantly be directing their children in godly living by doing all they can with their own testimonies and lifestyles.

Now what ... should a parent really look like?

Cultivating a godly parental model that emphasizes practical godliness

Intentional Parenting

Good parenting will not happen by chance or accident. Parents must realize they have guidelines in the instruction process, as found in Deuteronomy 6:5–7: "You shall love the LORD your God with all your heart and with all your soul and with all your might. And these words that I command you today shall be on your heart. You shall teach them diligently to your children, and shall talk of them when you sit in your house, and when you walk by the way, and when you lie down, and when you rise."

Servant Leaders

One of the most powerful influences a dad can have in the training of his children is in loving his wife and being quick and eager to serve her. Scriptural principles, whether applied at home, in the church, or elsewhere, emphasize service. God's Word shows clearly that the greatest leader is the servant-leader. Unfortunately, this trait is seldom displayed, though it may be spoken of easily. God's Word shows how valuable a cup of cold water is when one gives it in Christ's name; it is as if it was handed right to Him. In a family structure, the dad should be the one who takes this lead. He must desire, above all else, to serve whomever and whenever he can. Seldom, if ever, should he be the one asking for items; rather he should be asking others what their needs are and then see how he can best fulfill them.

Exposure to Many Things

It is important to present many options to children in all

circumstances. To simply expose them to interests of your own, and keep them from things you don't prefer, harms their overall development. God has created all people "fearfully and wonderfully," and, therefore to best further the refining of your "fearfully and wonderfully made" child, many opportunities should be embraced. Just because a child is not initially interested or accomplished in what he or she is being exposed to, parents should not discontinue the exposure. Interests to be considered can revolve around sports, music, art, nature, or travel, to name just a few.

As time continues, your child will begin to develop his or her own interests and skills around fewer items, but the initial idea should be to make sure there is exposure to many different areas, a few of which will become interests and passions. Financial resources are always a consideration. The intent is not to overspend what God has entrusted, but to choose wisely how best to influence and invest in your child and your child's future.

When One Expects Something, He Must Inspect It As Well!

It is easier to write down a list of expectations than it is to actually ensure that they are met. That is the next important aspect of the parenting pattern: following through and making sure that children are consistently adhering to the expectations laid out and that parents are doing the same by following through with the expected disciplinary measures.

As mentioned earlier, within the context of parenting, the expectations set will be difficult to identify and agree upon, but even more difficult is the follow-through when the child does not obey. Therefore, it is important to realize what obedience must look like

It is extremely important that parents realize that child-rearing is a "full time" responsibility. It is a twenty-four- hours-a-day, seven-days-a-week task. But the rewards of parenting will far outweigh the repeated sacrifices as you help your children reach their potential in every aspect of their life.

What's Best for My Child: Responsibility

Parents will always want the best for their children so, when it comes to gifts or opportunities, they are often eager to go beyond what they can afford. Teaching a child responsibility is far more valuable than anything money can buy or offer. Following through with a responsibility is, unfortunately, all too rare. The responsibility may be one that is of interest and easily attainable to the child. That is a great way to begin this training process. Giving a child the responsibility to bring the newspaper to a parent or to play with the dog may be easy to do and easy to recognize and reward. However, if the child doesn't like the responsibility he's given, and it is removed from his requirements, he learns that the only time he is required to work hard is when he wants to.

One of the greatest lessons a child can learn comes through being disciplined if he does not follow through with a task. In a way, this indicates a task may be completed without there being wholehearted work. Life is not made up of coasting through easy or enjoyable tasks. No wonder snooze buttons are placed on alarm clocks and people are given "grace" periods—people don't initially like to do things exactly when they are to do so. There is nothing wrong with not liking a given responsibility, but there is a lot wrong with not following through with what must be done.

Follow-through: Keeping Promises

Parents, teach this to your children and do so in word and deed! When your child needs something, and you as a parent promise to take care of that need, then no matter what is going on in your child's life, you as the parent must do so, and on time! There will be those times when you make mistakes and fail to follow through, but, when that happens, forgiveness needs to be sought and the issue confronted and resolved. There will be times that the promise is not kept because of other important issues taking place. But it is still imperative for your child to know that his or her interests are important enough for you as the parent to take note and realize you may have failed to keep a promise.

Mom and Dad Have to Obey, Too!

Not only is it important that children are disciplined, but it is just as important that parents are disciplined as well. One of the biggest inconsistencies in parenting is the expectations that parents place on their children which they, in turn, do not fulfill. Parents should be sure they are actually listening to the Word of God as it is presented to them in its spoken and written forms. Then, they should listen to the expectations they give their children. They should be sure that they are following through with the rules as well as aiming to achieve the same kinds of goals in their own lives as they expect of their children,. If children are expected not to lie, then parents must consistently follow through with what they tell them. The list can go on and on, but, suffice it to say, if God's Word says it, then mom and dad better do it. In that way, they are then licensed to expect this from their children.

If parents expect a child to obey the authorities, then they, too, should be willing to submit to those who have responsibility over them. This will be in the form of pastors, government representatives, and work supervisors. If the parents speak derogatorily about those who have authority over them, they are only teaching their child to be that way toward his authority. It is an easy mistake for parents to be critical of the authorities to which they, as adults, are meant to be in submission, and yet to discipline their children for having insubordinate spirits!

It must be underscored that parents should also be careful that they do follow through with the promises they make. When a child has asked repeatedly for someone to play with, or read to him or her, it is easy, without thinking, to say that one will do that "later" or "tomorrow." This will appease the child for the moment, but when the child realizes that the "later" or "tomorrow" has never occurred, the parent has actually lied! It is necessary for the parents to be sure their words are spoken as if they are sharing them with a colleague or peer. Following through with what is stated to a child is even more important than following through with others. Too often, though, parents want to be more careful with those who really aren't as important as that child they are discipling.

When you rise up, and when you lie down, and when you walk about ...

God clearly states that parents are to be living examples before their children. According to Deuteronomy 6:6–7—"And these words that I command you today shall be on your heart. You shall teach them diligently to your children, and shall talk of them when you sit in your house, and when you walk by the way, and when you lie down, and when you rise."—parents are to be directing their children to love God with their lives as well as their words. Parents are to constantly be directing their children in godly living by doing all they can with their own testimonies and lifestyles.

A great directive is to be sure that "when one walks by the way" (that is, the normal flow of daily living), godly living is taking place. Scriptural teaching is easy to hear and say, but so much harder to live out in practice. What is heard on Sunday must be lived Monday through Saturday! When children are getting up in the morning, although not everyone is a "morning person," they are still to be conscientious and Christlike. This must not only be taught by the parents, but must also be implemented by them as well! They should be careful that they are not just relying on a caffeine boost from their coffee for this! Finally, when one lies down, that time helps us to realize we can be thankful to God for all He has done with the day, no matter what the blessings or disappointments.

It is easy to decide that each family will have a "devotional time" during the day. This requires everyone to get together and have a short lesson for consideration. That is a great idea, but one should be careful it does not only breed a theoretical kind of faith—one which has people saying the right thing during the time of devotions, but then going out and living inconsistently with those things that have been discussed. The best way to rear children is as God instructs in this passage in Deuteronomy—to be sure godly instruction and lifestyles are consistently practiced all day, every day.

What does that "nurture and admonition of the Lord" mean?

Bringing children up in the nurture and admonition—the "discipline and instruction" (ESV)—of the Lord is critically important. Everyone needs a foundation for what to do and why to do it. Likewise, using the Bible as the resource for what is done is also of critical importance. Parents often want to know how soon to begin potty training and when a child should speak in complete sentences. Those issues are not specifically listed in Scripture. What is listed in Scripture is that all are to love God with their whole heart, soul, mind, and strength, and, secondarily, to love their neighbor as themselves. When these principles are implemented, a child will also begin to follow the commands of "Delight yourself in the LORD, and he will give you the desires of your heart." (Psalm 37:4) and "but seek first the kingdom of God and his righteousness, and all these things will be added to you" (Matthew 6:33).

A child must be taught how to love God. At an early age, he should be continually presented with the gospel as well as discipled by the gospel. An unregenerate heart will not be able to do what is right. A person may be able to do what is relatively good, but not always what is absolutely right. To be holy, as God expects us to strive to be, requires following His standard. The guidelines for knowing God are given throughout His Word. Since God said in the New Testament, (Matthew 22:37–29) that on the two commands given in the previous paragraph hangs all of the law and the prophets, consider how important those truths really are. If one will love God as he ought, then he will never want to go against God's command. That's why it is so vitally important for a child to be taught God's Word from a very early age. If an early age was not the time this was addressed, then perhaps some "catching up" will have to be done to be sure one is correctly being directed for God's glory. Either way, though, parents must strive to give children God's truths.

If one will love God, and know his commands, then to truly love Him requires true obedience to Him! If a child will obey God as he ought, then he will have proper attitudes and will not lie; he will be kind to others and be forgiving in his spirit. If he truly loves others as he loves himself, then he will never be selfish or prideful in his dealings with others. Using this as a guideline is so much more straightforward than teaching sons how to fish or teaching daughters how to sew! Fishing and sewing are certainly good skills to have, but they don't make one obey God any more if they are done one way or the other. If a child is always frustrated at his situation, then he is not living as God commanded, which is to be content always.

Why Is My Attitude So Important?

You must esteem others better than yourself. This is not only necessary in the work force or while dating, but even even when caring for an infant. Never let your children hear you respond negatively to your spouse, or even in frustration at the recurrence of their behavior. Your children are still to be considered "better than yourself." This practice should be consistently followed throughout the course of their upbringing. You may want to consider children as "people in process." How you direct them, and influence them, and are an example to them at the pressure moments of life, will go a long way in helping them learn how to respond to life's events in either a godly or godless manner.

I can recall early on in our marriage when I raised my voice inappropriately at my wife. At that exact moment, our dog, which had been reprimanded in his past, went slinking out of the room. Attitude, volume, and harshness may not have been directed at the animal, but the manner certainly was understood. That rebuke has stayed with me all these years!

What Do I Do When Things Go Wrong?

No matter what the difficulty, it is of vital importance that the parent always praises God and has an optimistic "trust in God" attitude. No matter how many times a difficulty occurs, or the situation doesn't seem possible in its recovery, God expects people to rejoice in Him consistently—they are to "rejoice always" (1 Thessalonians 5:16). When a parent consistently displays this attitude, a child can easily determine that all that is ever done can be brought into a rejoicing experience. It is always important to remember that the rejoicing is to be "always!" There are many times that children will respond appropriately and accordingly to rules and expectations. There will also be many times when the variety of life's events will flow and be special and encouraging. However, at those times when obedience is not occurring, and other difficulties have happened, Christlike behavior will be fostered, not by teaching, but by example.

Wisdom from God's Word

Fathers, provoke not your children to wrath, but bring them up in the nurture and admonition of the Lord. (Ephesians 6:4)

It is extremely important to follow all of God's commands, but there doesn't seem to be one that is harder to fulfill than this. There are always going to be differences of opinions and failures as parents. God does expect people to pattern their lives after Christ's perfect example. The intent of the perfection is to follow Christ's perfect example and always to be seeking to be all that one can be for His glory.

This kind of provoking—provoking your children to wrath— happens when rules and expectations change, not to mention the follow-through of the discipline for improper behavior. Therefore, since you as a parent aren't going to be perfect, you are inevitably going to disappoint and frustrate your children during your parenting days. When you give proper biblical commands and follow through with proper discipline, at times that may bring about differences of opinions. So you must be very quick to be sure you are doing all you can to keep from changing expectations and trying to impose your own desires on your children rather than what God requires. When children are following parental authority and make mistakes, as a parent you shouldn't take it upon yourself to bring even more punishment upon them—not to mention the withdrawing of love during these times. Simply put, provoking should not occur, and it won't if you are following through with your own set of biblical mandates of godly living.

> *Husbands, love your wives, even as Christ Jesus loved the church!*
> *(Ephesians 5:25)*

This truth is taught from the pulpit and in Sunday School, but if it is not lived out in the home, it will be a mute point and never followed by young men. It is of even greater importance that what is taught is also caught! It is extremely important that a dad will kindly and compassionately care for and show kindness to his wife. This occurs when he tries to "lay down his life for her" and serve her in all ways. Too many husbands lord over their spouses their "prominent" role of being the leader, as laid out in Scripture, and fail in being the servant-leader Christ exemplified. According to God's Word, paralleling Christ's love for the church reveals a love that was not deserved, but nevertheless needed. It is so easy, and natural, to love when one is loved.

Anyone can do that! To truly love when one is not loved, or when one is hurt, shows true humility and Christlikeness.

Wives, submit to your own husbands, as to the Lord. (Ephesians 5:22)

It is vitally important to reflect on Christ's Word when submitting. Putting yourself in subjection to another person is not even easy when everything is going well! So, when issues are not being handled biblically and the flesh raises its ugly head, submitting to your husband will be very difficult. At those times it is imperative to realize that the submission is actually to God, and the husband just happens to be in the "way" and receives the submission.

Too many wives say they would submit if they had someone worthy of submitting to. However, according to this verse, God is the one they are to be submitting to, so they need to realize they should submit, regardless of the fairness of the circumstances of their life. To truly be Christlike in their situation is to submit in just the same manner as Christ submitted in the garden when he said, "Not my will, but yours, be done" (Luke 22:42). Although truth would allow parents to teach a child without patterning it in their own lives, it will not do any good in the overall parenting plan if they themselves do not exemplify these same values and lifestyles as well. It is imperative to train children in accordance with God's Word. While doing so, it is just as important for them to do so in a godly way. For example, one should not lose one's temper while repeating verbal instructions, as that only confuses the instruction.

Some Other Things to Think About

You have to be together to have together time!

Doing things together as a family is of vital importance. One of the best ways to spend time together as a family is to try to commit to being together for at least one meal a day. This sounds so simple when a child is newborn. In fact, every mealtime seems to have the family together when you have an infant. But as schedules change and school and work gradually become more demanding, it will become harder and harder to be together in the normal working of events. As the family gets older and each child in turn takes on more responsibilities and enjoys more opportunities, one has to work harder to keep this structure in place. And, the time may not be very long, as people have to part ways to fulfill other responsibilities. Do not ever underestimate the value of time spent together.

Another valuable time together is when engaging in activities. It is critically important as a family to create and share memories. This may take the form of a recital, ball game, or school activity. Make sure it is not considered a chore or drudgery to be together. Make the times fun. Playing board games is a tremendous way to spend time together. There may be many occasions that a conversation will not take place with the family just sitting in the living room, but when all the family members are somewhat occupied attending to a game, guards may be dropped and some conversations naturally and spontaneously develop that never would have taken place had an activity not been suggested and enjoyed. As the saying goes, "It does take quantity time to get quality time."

Giving each child an option to choose what the family will do in a thirty-minute time slot can make for a special block of time as each one chooses a specific request, and the family all participates in that.

Another special way to spend time together is for you as a parent to carve out a specified time with each family member, perhaps thirty minutes each. That time is spent alone with your son or daughter and it could be spent just conversing or sharing.

Your only quiet time may be with God

Children need to know that mom and dad spend time with God. This doesn't have to be discussed and displayed as it is easy for them to observe how parents live throughout the day. If parents are patient and kind, encouraging and comforting, then the child knows that a devotional life occurs. This is also a great time for parents to speak of God's goodness and holiness as they walk in the way, sit down, and rise up! (Deuteronomy 6:7).

It is extremely important to have this quiet time with the Lord. Not only does God's Word command it, but life will demand it. It is better to prepare for an action than for a reaction. One must practice often to develop a habit. If a parent wants to habitually be known for his Christlike behavior, then he will need to get to know God in a very intimate and personal way. He will need to continually feed on the principles which God's Word affords.

Just like breakfast helps to start a day, so can a time with the Lord. Depending upon your personality and life clock, it may not be feasible for you to have your time with the Lord in the morning. The important aspect of this is to continually be imbibing God's principles and precepts. As you feed on God's Word, daily habits will become engrained. It will be because of these habits that you, as a parent, will be able to react appropriately to your children and to life's difficulties in a proper and godly manner.

Take the time to share what took place in your devotional time. It doesn't have to be a lengthy discourse on every verse read, but it is important to periodically share a special and spiritual thought that God gave you through the reading. One talks about what is important, and when God and His Word and ways are important, then it will be often discussed and shared. It is also a great way to help your children speak about God in a practical and personal way.

Let's get out of here!—or, To be (gone) or not to be (gone) …

God has entrusted your children to you for the express purpose of allowing you to bring them into a gospel-centered lifestyle. There are many life events which children will encounter that are important for them to learn without their parents necessarily involved. The first and most important human relationship in a family is that of the husband and wife. Even though a child is the most wonderful human event that has occurred in the life of a marriage, the child is not to take the place of one parent's first love for his or her spouse. There is nothing wrong with parents jointly caring for their child and offering sacrifice of time and energy in the follow-through with all of the responsibilities associated with that upbringing.

One of the greatest gifts parents can give each other is the time to again be just husband and wife. This can occur in a variety of ways. Be sure that your time alone is special. Create such an atmosphere in your bedroom that you both feel it is a haven from a busy day and a time to again recount and express love to each other. Even if there is only fifteen minutes of alone time before both of you crash from a busy day, it is still special to know there is a connecting time when no other cares are around.

One way to be sure this happens is to make sure your bedroom is a special place. There will, of course, be times when clothes stay around and out in the room, or some remodeling project may have to stay in sight. On a regular basis, however, the room should normally be as welcoming as if guests were coming over and might happen to see it. How you spend your fifteen spare minutes can go a long way in keeping that special bond and relationship for the less pressurized times when you can spend more than those short minutes.

Another great way to continue the special relationship between husband and wife is to go away for a time. It may just be as simple as going out for a brief dessert, or an overnight getaway. One can't always be going away as life doesn't afford that, and neither, probably, can you! Having a time that can be reflected on as "another honeymoon" makes the many moments and days, when you never think you'll be alone again, to not only be endured but enjoyed! When these occasions can be enjoyed, make sure that you don't spend your time "missing" your child or family. In other words, make sure these times are for the joy of each other, as family life will be waiting for you when you return. It may be a good time to reflect on how you are doing as parents and to consider goals which were set. However, it should not be a time that is spent missing your children; you will soon be back with them, and will then be missing the short time that you had alone with your marriage partner! Make sure that the time is directly enjoyed with your spouse. Go back in your relationship and reminisce on the many ways you were drawn together and recount the joys of love and affection that you have and share. Bible books such as The Song of Solomon and certain verses in Proverbs highlight the physical relationship and the joy which can be derived through the gift God gave in that regard. Those times aren't going to occur as often as either of you want if you don't have special times away.

Because life will be made up of times apart, learn to enjoy the times you are apart so you can enjoy the times you are again together. When children go to someone else's home, don't tell them you'll miss them, but share with them that you love them and will look forward to seeing them again. Don't forget, you are rearing your children to spend most of their lives apart from you. Allow this lesson to be an easy transition rather than a stark reality when they are much older. Remind yourself of this when you as a husband or wife have additional responsibilities that take you apart from each other. If true love is evident, there will definitely be a tug on the heart of missing the other. The time apart should be spent doing things which couldn't have been done quite as easily, or with the same duration, as it could be when you are together. Enjoy the time apart and then the together time is even sweeter!

This lesson was so evident when my wife experienced our first child being separated from us. Until she was weaned, mom was with daughter on a continuous basis. And that was a good thing. Without mentioning it to my wife, I found a means for us to get away for an overnight excursion. There was not much expense and not much time, but alone time was so rare at that stage that it seemed too good to be true. However, my wife had other ideas when I excitedly told her of the plan! She was almost upset that I could have thought to have done such a thing. Figuratively, and perhaps even literally, I had to drag her "kicking and screaming" from her firstborn.

Implementing the practice of not spending our time speaking about our child was hard at first, but it began to have its way. As time would have it, the short excursion was over. Thinking that the opposite would now be true—that my wife would excitedly be heading back to pick up her baby—was reversed when I had to drag her "kicking and screaming" when we had to return! That experience proved how strong a love can be for one's child, but how much stronger that love should be, and can be, for the first love produced by the marriage bond.

Young parents, and couples in general, should get away for times together and shouldn't spend time talking about children, unless that's the agenda. Rather, they should spend time discussing their interests and excitements. They will find that if they keep the joy prior to having children while they are rearing children, the "empty nest" will still be a fulfilled one with the spouse of their youth!

Being a parent is going to be so easy—my mom and dad made it seem so simple.
The only reason "mom and dad" made it seem easy was because all of the frustrating years are so far behind them and grown children are able to be the "fruit of their labors." When parents are constantly crying out to the Lord for their needs, in the light of the counsel of James 1:5—"If any of you lacks wisdom, let him ask God, who gives generously to all without reproach, and it will be given him."—children don't often see this pursuit for God's help.

Establishing rules for my marriage and family
It is best to establish procedures which are implemented when conflict develops in relationships in the family. You should decide early on that the mom-dad relationship takes first priority. There should never be a side of the discipline that is any different if dad is in charge or if mom is. All planning in advance, for disciplinary purposes, should be a joint decision. At times there may be some discussion, and even disagreement, when these are first brought out and discussed. However, when the decisions

are finally being implemented, there must be total agreement on the parenting side of the equation. Mom and dad are always on the same side. They will have different personalities and will act and react differently. They will both have certain areas that they are more interested in developing in their children. That is why it is so important, from the beginning, that parents understand the importance of considering how they should, as a couple, rear their child for God's glory. As long as they have the same end-goal, they will be able to focus on working toward that end as they must consider their different perspectives, yet keeping in view the ultimate goal of pleasing God.

So What Do You Do for Fun?

One of the biggest areas of "fun" for any family is finding something that each member will enjoy doing together with other family members. There will, of course, be hobbies that each parent has. One great way for there to be a cohesion in family interests is if mom and dad have found something that they enjoy doing together. As the years proceed, the children naturally begin to enjoy what they are being exposed to. Exposure is one of the easiest ways for hobbies to be encountered and enjoyed. It is difficult, though, to be sure to take time to gradually help your children enjoy your family's hobby. You and your spouse will need to be patient with them, and ease them into the exposure. Since you have already enjoyed this, you are undoubtedly quite accomplished or at least have a love for the activity. The key to the family activity is that all members participate, as it will add wonderful memories for many years to come. When parents don't initially like something a child suggests, but eagerly get involved, it shows the importance of really enjoying each other and the worth the other person has. Parents can be very quick to desire and demand that a child participates in what their interests are, but it can be another story when they should be getting involved in their children's interests.

Now I know what Mary must have felt like …

Mary was mother to a perfect Son—and she must have been overwhelmed with that thought. She was imperfect but her Son was perfect. Although He was perfect, God chose to have Him reared by imperfect people. God knew that it must have been an overwhelming task but He wanted us not only to receive a Savior in the Person of His Son, but also to view that He would have humans capable of rearing His Son. If they could do that, they could also rear their own.

"Mom" encompasses so many details. She has given birth to the child and wants nothing more than that her baby receives all of the love and care available. She is the encourager, support group, and the one displaying the most compassion and sympathy in the home. She also wants to be sure that the most important aspect of her mothering is that she supports her husband in the discipline of the children. She and her husband may not always be in agreement as to the exact nature of the upbringing of their child, but she will work together with her husband, and want to be a consistent help, in every aspect.

Being mom to an infant is going to be different than being mom to a teenager. In many cases, a mom may be that to both ages at the same time. Having one child, or ten, does not lessen the responsibility to do all she can to help each child be all that he or she can be for God's glory. According to Scripture, there is no set of rules that tell you what exactly you are to do. The most important command, or "rule," is to personally love the Lord with all your heart and then your neighbor as yourself (see Matthew 22:37–40). As you display your love for God by always being and doing what you should for His glory, and as you faithfully support and encourage your husband and love your children, they will see what is expected of a Christian, and want to follow that example. You will make mistakes as pressures build and disappointments arise. As a godly mom should do, work as hard as you can to love and serve as you believe God would have you, and when you make a serious mistake, readily admit that, both to God and those in your family against whom you may have sinned. That will not only keep your relationship what it should be but will also reveal to them how they can be released from their wrongdoing, for if they have parents with genuinely human qualities, they, in turn, will act similarly.

If you are a mom, the worst thing you can do is to allow fear to paralyze you in your role of being mom and to stop doing what you believe is best—especially as you may have made mistakes in your past. Realizing it is an extremely important role to fill, and that God entrusted your child to you, will only determine how important it is and how you will continue to follow up on requirements and expectations.

So I Must Obey ... But What Do I Obey?

When it comes to obedience, one doesn't need a huge book of rules. The following are the expectations in child-rearing: Children should always obey their authority, always respect others, and never lie. These should be the reasons children are noted for obedience or disobedience. It can, at times, be easy to discipline because parents are embarrassed or angry.

The simpler rules, the easier it is to implement them. Rather than deciding on a long list of rules, begin thinking along the lines of expectations. As these expectations become clearer, the list of "rules" will develop. At the same time, the importance of expectations in the home is that they should be followed completely. Whatever is expected from the parents is a requirement. Failure to follow this will result in the child being disciplined.

Here is an example of how discipline may take place when a parent has allowed something to get out of hand. It's a practical example like this: There is a rule stating that no beverage is to be taken into the white-carpeted living room. A child will periodically take a glass of water in there and, although it was stated that no beverage was to be taken, there is no discipline or reprimand. This occurs at first guardedly, for the child remembers and knows what the rule was. As the rule is passively administered, the child continues to periodically disobey. While there is no application of discipline, it is easy for the child to be comfortable that the rule must not be in effect any more. On one occasion, red Kool-Aid is taken into the living room but, since no spills occur, still nothing is done about the offense. Finally, the red beverage is spilled and the parents become angry about the disobedient behavior, and they discipline the child promptly.

The problem with this is that the parents are only disciplining now because their white carpet has a red stain on it! They are not disciplining because the beverage was taken into the room—and yet that is where the most important correction should have taken place.

Help! Which Way Do I Go?

Remember, God's Word commands parents to train up a child in the way he should go! That means that the child is to be directed to follow the course of his own personality and talents, and not to become exactly as his parents may want him to be. If God clothes the lilies of the field, and knows when sparrows fall to the ground (see Matthew 6:30 and 10:29), He knows how to bring children to Himself and keep them developing in the path of life that would most bring glory to Him. Children will not always make the wisest of decisions and, as has been stated, they are to have very specific commands early on in their life to learn many of these principles. As they mature, however, the specific and exact statements may not be as many, but the heartfelt direction is still there. When a child likes something, even though it may not be what the parents like, as long as it is not violating the principles of obedience and godliness, then the child should be encouraged to follow through with that.

During the phase of helping the child find his or her "natural bent," a parent should continually desire to assist the child in knowing what is right and wrong about their involvement.

Being a Role Model

It is not only important to be a proper God-honoring dad for the purpose of being obedient in this role, but it is also a motivating factor to realize children can, and will, pattern their marital choices and lifestyles after their parents. A dad should be a positive role model because his daughters will see him and determine the godly characteristics in his life and desire those in their husbands. He will also be a role model for his sons to emulate in their future roles as fathers.

Likewise, a mom should be a positive role model because her sons will see her and determine the godly characteristics in her life and desire those in their wives. She should also be a proper role model for her daughters for them to emulate in their future roles as mothers.

It is also important that young people realize that how they act as young people will affect how they act as adults. The way a young man treats his mom parallels the way he will treat his wife. How a young woman treats her dad parallels the manner in which she will treat her husband. How young people respect and honor their parents will parallel how they respect and honor their spouses one day.

A glimpse into this chapter . . .

Be sure that you spend time with your children before bedtime, especially when they are young. Let them know that you are so committed to them and their wellbeing that you are prepared to put aside your adult projects to be with them. Love your time with them, even if you have a lot of things to do after you get them to bed. Just like every child is different, so is every stage of a child's life. The development of individuals will not track perfectly, but the following will give some idea of what are some important considerations to be made while rearing a child.

Teaching a child about using the restroom is yet another important part of the growing up years. It is neither an easy task, nor is it one always easily learned. It is important, though, to balance appropriately the thought of obedience and function.

Realizing that God created sex means that it is good. It is only through the improper display of activities outside of the marriage bed (see Hebrews 13:4) that one begins to associate sex with improper behavior.

Parents are given the wonderful, awesome, and overwhelming responsibility to rear their children as God would have them reared. It is now time to pray with and enjoy your children as they continue in that which they have been taught. They will undoubtedly do things differently, and may even vacillate in what they do from decision to decision. They are simply trying to do what they believe to be best.

Now what... are the stages in child-rearing?

Navigating wisely through the ages and stages that lead to adulthood

Night-Night

B e sure that you spend time with your children before bedtime, especially when they are young. Let them know that you are so committed to them and their well-being that you are prepared to put aside your adult projects to be with them. Love your time with them, even if you have a lot of things to do after you get them to bed. Bedtime can be a sweet time. It is the end of their day, and undoubtedly not the end of yours. Allow them a little time to talk or ask questions, yet without allowing them to manipulate their bedtime.

Rest is vitally important for young children. They seem energetic and could keep going a little later than you suggest for their bedtime. Although it can be tempting to put them to bed for your own peace and quiet, that is not the reason. Nor is the reason to let them stay up so you don't have to wrestle with them until they finally go to sleep. This is another difficult training time. Children are so precious when they are asleep, but, at times, to get them there really brings out the worst in both the parents and the child. This is unnecessary. Simply put, the rest for children is for their good and it will help in the proper development of their temples—that is, their bodies—for God's glory. One could go into all of the health and wellness secrets behind rest, but that is not the point of this discussion. The importance is for children to know that when they are told to do anything, they must obey, and based upon the four key points of obedience mentioned in Chapter 3 (remember when examined how Abraham obeyed God)—*immediately, completely, willingly* and *acceptably.*

They must obey in your putting them to bed. They are to be quiet, and still, and go to sleep. If they don't go to sleep right away, that is okay, as long as they are not crying and seeking attention. That is when you may have to discipline them. If they have had a full day of activities, and you have been keeping them on the go, they will fall asleep! If, however, they will not go to sleep, it is important to note whether they are obeying you completely in this aspect of training, too.

Once your children are in bed, the expectations could be, and should be, that they must lie still, keep their heads down, and be quiet. Playing some music quietly may assist in their calming as well. Children are not obeying if they do not conform to these three requirements. Children disobey when they do not lie still, keep their heads down, and keep quiet. If the parents have made certain to have the children in clean pajamas or diapers, and are sure that they have had all of their needs meet prior to going to bed, then there is nothing they need over the simple rule of rest. If they do protest by either rearing their head up, or continually calling for "mommy" or "daddy," then they are disobeying!

That is why it is so very important to have procedures in place in advance in case a child disobeys. Whatever has been decided upon as a means of discipline should be followed at this time as well. If the child has disobeyed, then the parent needs to follow through with the standard procedure, require the child to return to his bedtime protocol, and the parent should leave again. No matter how many times the child repeats his acts of disobedience, the parent should follow through with this very important aspect of training.

A child must not be allowed to get the upper hand in this area. If he does, it is just as wrong as his stealing or being disrespectful. Disobedience requires discipline. Here is a thought to continually help in the formation of disciplinary consequences: the pain of the discipline should far outweigh the pleasure of the disobedience.

Up Close and Personal—Potty Training

Teaching a child about using the restroom is yet another important part of the growing up years. It is neither an easy task, nor is it one always easily learned. It is important, though, to balance appropriately the thought of obedience and function. Initially, it will be important to help a child learn to use the bathroom so you won't continually have to use diapers. In the end, though, it is important to help the child learn this so he or she can function throughout life. It is simply another important area to train a child.

There will, at first, be "accidents" as this new discipline is learned. As time goes on, though, those "accidents" may be a symptom of rebellion. This is one of the hardest areas to be certain of. All children develop differently, and even within the same home this can be confusing. As the parents begin understanding their child and his newfound abilities, they must also recognize when their child is not doing what he should do. It's at those times that the parenting process continues in its importance and discipline may become necessary. Remember, the only reason for discipline is disobedience so, if a child knows what to do, and does not do so, then the sinful behavior needs correction.

It will be important to note that initially the boy or girl will have to be shown what is taking place in his or her body. This can begin even in the first year, but typically it is after sixteen to eighteen months. Girls seem to be the quicker learners. Be patient with this as they both develop in this delicate issue. Don't forget, they need to know this for the rest of their life! Don't just treat it as a task to endure and don't become frustrated when they don't follow through as they have been instructed. Let them know you are praying for them as they adjust to something new for them. It may not be understood, but your patience will help them realize you are more interested in them than you are in your schedule.

Preschool Years

This is the time of child-rearing that you are involved in the "telling" phase. This phase involves one-way communication with children and is typically used through the age of three or four. Children at this stage need clear direction and close supervision. Everything which is expected of a child is directly told him. An example which will be used is helping a child get ready for bed. In this phase, the parent will tell the child every aspect of this discipline—right down to the detailed instructions to "take out and change into your pajamas, brush your teeth, get into bed."

When a mom is nursing her child, she might as well be the

one who gets up in the night, as there is really not much else the dad can do. However, once the child needs some help in the night, her husband ought to be the one who gets up. That gives the dad extra time with the child, as well as being a help to the mom who has the full-time duty during the day.

The preschool years are often a time when children are considered quite a nuisance. Yet this is the best training period of their lives. They will not remember the countless times of discipline and reinforcement and will be best suited to learn what they are to do for God's glory. Give them expectations which are positive and optimistic. Rather than considering these times as, for example, the "terrible twos" etc., consider them the "tremendous twos, the thrilling threes, the fabulous fours, and the fantastic fives." Parental attitudes will go a long way in eliciting a child's best response.

Kindergarten/Elementary Years

In this time frame, you teach—give them instruction—give them some time to make sure they understand what you have told them. When teaching, you will instruct your child to do something he is capable of doing by using two-way question-and-answer communication.

Using our "getting ready for bed" example, you tell them to go to bed and then you ask them what that means they are to do. Their answer, if you have trained them in such a way, would be to first get dressed for bed. You next examine if they actually did get dressed for bed on their own. Then you ask what they are to do next and they will state that they are to brush their teeth, lay out clothes for the following day, and go to bed. You'll follow through with the same pattern as before, with the question-and-answer method, along with examination of the same. They are given the opportunity to be told that they are to get ready for bed, but they will still be reminded about the next step if it is forgotten.

Up Close and Personal—Sex Education

Realizing that God created sex means that it is good. It is only through the improper display of activities outside of the marriage bed (see Hebrews 13:4) that one begins to associate sex with improper behavior. God has created man and woman to be appealing in many areas and the respective make up of each is one noticeable difference. Since God has stated in The Song of Solomon and Proverbs some very graphic details about the enjoyment of sex, and has tempered this with the marriage union, then an extremely easy means of guiding children in this very tempting area is that they are to *act* married only when they *are* married. As The Song of Solomon states, "My beloved is mine, and I am his ..." (Song of Solomon 2:16) Within marriage, that is proper and to be followed.

Parents should allow their children to direct their conversations about sex. Early in a child's life, such questions as "How are babies made?" and "Where do babies come from?" are likely to be asked. Parents should answer the questions appropriately to their age. When children are at about the age of ten or eleven, parents should begin telling them about their bodies, and the differences experienced by both sexes. This can be linked initially with the leading questions of the child, and it may well eventually become a planned discussion of God's creation of man and woman, and the sexual union blessed by God. Truth, like God created it, is the perfect way of helping children realize they are "fearfully and wonderfully made" (Psalm 139:14) and this includes the physical makeup of their potential future marital union.

At some point and time (my wife and I did this on our daughters' and sons' sixteenth birthdays), it may be a great moment of sealing in their minds the importance of remaining a virgin until they are married by giving them a "purity" symbol. (In our case, we gave each child a ring.) This is a constant reminder to them of "not acting married until they are married."

Late Elementary/Junior High Years

In this phase, a child will begin to be taught using the participating method. This is the time you are involved as a player-coach. Proper behavior is communicated more by example and interaction and less by direct instruction. Parental control decreases as you encourage your child to learn and make decisions and carry out behavior on his own. The parent will begin guiding the child when another event is about to occur, but the liberty will be given for the decision on how to follow through with the ensuing responsibilities.

Using the earlier example, the child is told to get ready for bed. He may decide to brush his teeth first, and then change clothes and get into bed. The final goal is that he is in bed and on time. If his thinking and performing occurs in a different order, but the same final outcome occurs, then that is acceptable. However, if the child cannot function within the guidelines of performing a designated task with the proper final outcome, then this participation method may need to reverse to the teaching method of the earlier elementary years. Once the child advances beyond that, there can be more flexibility and he can begin to have more responsibilities within the obedience framework.

Beginning with the junior high years, often peer pressure begins to mount. Doing what others may desire or consider appropriate can be considered good or bad. It just depends upon what type of pressure is being applied. If it is the type of peer pressure Daniel suggested about his friends, in doing what God wanted, this is good. You want your child to have the right type of friends to be influenced properly. When you begin to note improper attitudes and behaviors, consider what friendships they are beginning to establish. Encourage them to discontinue their friendships with those who are a bad influence and to seek to develop friendships with those who provide a healthy influence. This is a great time to begin having your child's friends into your home. Simply noting how they respond to your authority and how they relate to the other children in your home will go a long way in determining whether you want them as a friend to your child. If they are engaging in the home, properly responsive to authority, and kind to your other children in your home, you have found a good friend for your child. On the other hand, if they are negative in all of the above, then it is imperative you make proper decisions about who influences your child.

Another great way to consider this is to make sure your child is being the right kind of influence as well. The same principles stated before about what type of friends your child has should be followed by him as well.

High School Years

This is the time parents begin empowering their children to think for themselves. This is when you begin delegating more independence to them. It is the final step toward your child's maturity. You have now moved to the state of reciprocal giving and receiving. It is used with mature preteens and adolescents, able and willing to take responsibility and perform tasks on their own.

Consider the following example. Rather than telling your teen exactly what is to be done, you will rather state an expectation, and let him or her determine what is necessary to make sure that occurs. For example, you may decide, and tell your teen, what time you are leaving the next day for school. He or she will determine, by assessing what needs to be done in the morning prior to the departure time, and will set an alarm to wake up at the right time, get ready for and into bed independently—with no need to be woken up the next morning! (Of course, in the event of oversleeping, the lesson of actions and consequences will occur if expectations are not followed through.)

At this final state, your child will probably make decisions differently than you do and his conclusions will be different from yours. This is the evidence of maturity and independence. However, the same and proper obedience must occur. The expectations you have for your child must be fulfilled. If they are done in a different manner and sequence, that is okay. If they are not followed at all, then you should revisit the previous phase and review some of the responsibilities.

Consider the apostle Peter: his name meant "rock." When Christ first called Peter to follow Him, He called him Simon. When Peter himself began to realize his potential, Christ called him Peter. Peter was known for his impetuous and improper behavioral choices and actions. He was also known for many right choices. Because of his potential, God gave him his new name of Peter. This example may be a great thought for children in their upbringing. Consider what potential they have, and teach and discipline toward that. Not all of the plans for their life are certain, but the fact that they will follow God will do wonders in their overall objectives. By setting goals and demands of the same, one is merely recognizing that they are not settling for something trivial and easy, but important and demanding.

Peer Pressure

At this time of life, there will be many times when your child will want to have his or her own course of action and desire to exercise his or her own rights. These are the times that you remind your child that you have been investing much time, talent, and treasure into his or her life. It is because of this, and not because you expect any remuneration, that you are so cautious and hesitant at times. It is because you want him or her to fulfill the purpose for which you have been rearing him or her—that is, to get the full value of your investment.

Modesty

Many people discuss, and are divided, as to how to instruct and monitor modesty. 1 Corinthians 6:12–20 gives significant direction on how Christians are to live in accordance with the holiness of God. Children are to realize that they are to obey and honor their parents, so initially they may wear only what their parents provide and permit. At the same time, as children are growing, it is the wisest course of action to instill in them the standards and practices that will stay with them throughout the course of life.

Principles provided in 1 Corinthians 6 address the fact that one's body is not one's own, but God's. Because of that, it is imperative that your children clothe their bodies in such a way as to bring glory to God rather than attention to themselves. So, if they will follow God's law, and your instructions, they will never go wrong. From a human standpoint, it helps them to establish the principles of being above reproach and of wearing apparel appropriate to the particular occasion. Thus the detail of the decision becomes easy to work out from a principled point of view. Your children must be encouraged to be honest with themselves and not fall to the standards of their friends or of the society in which they live, realizing, rather, that they must seek to please the Lord in the matter of the occasion or setting in which they plan to wear the garment.

College Years

The parent and child at this time are in a very different position. The child has been encouraged throughout his or her life to be getting ready to leave the home and make decisions alone. The parent is still the authority, so when issues are raised which require parental control, the parent must require obedience. However, it is very important that the parent remembers the empowerment factor and decides that fewer and fewer issues need to be under such control. Using the bedtime example at this stage would mean that the parent asks questions to simply know what is going on for vehicle usage or combining and coordinating schedules.

This is a great time of encouragement for the young adult. Discussions about life plans and goals and pursuits are very important. Parents should make it a point to discuss many situations with their child, and determine what decisions are being made, and why they are being made. Just because they are being done differently isn't wrong; it is just information so both can understand and encourage each other better.

It is vitally important that children are continually being directed to make decisions for themselves, but, at the same time, they are to maintain proper decisions. As a general rule, once they have commenced a course of study, young adults should stay in college. One of the greatest tests of faith and practice is finishing what has been set out. Wonderful Christian maturing begins when it is hard to do a task. Another great aspect of college is being alone, and relying on God.

This is the final phase to assist children in moving from dependence on parents to semi-dependence, and finally dependence on God. God does want children to be independent and free, so they can worship and serve Him on their own. He does want them to be obedient in their pursuits and plans. They need to desire to live according to the principles that have already been set out in the parenting times, and, if followed, the child will be doing what God wants. They may not eventually seek the major or path their parents had wanted, and that is just fine. However, if they are not willing to seek God's kingdom first (see Matthew 6:33), then there is something wrong.

Adult Years

These are the years following a child's college training. There are those times that adult children will graduate, become gainfully employed, but are not yet married. The role changes somewhat if and when marriage takes place. If parents will entrust their child into the holy union of marriage, then they must realize that all of their parenting in regards to discipline is complete. The Bible is clear in its teaching that "... a man shall leave his father and his mother and hold fast to his wife, and they shall become one flesh" (Genesis 2:24).

Parents are now in the advisory role. They may at times be asked for this and at other times may feel compelled to offer it. There is nothing wrong with giving parental advice, but parents must be aware that advice doesn't have to be heeded to have been heard. One of the greatest gifts God gives us is the conviction of the Holy Spirit. When God works, that is sufficient. Parents, although their concern is appropriate and evident, are not the child's authority any more. The couple—that is, the husband as the head of his bride—are now responsible to God for their actions and decisions. Prayer is such a powerful tool and patience in counsel is one of the greatest gifts that can be given. Leaving the results to their children and their God will ease both the parents in their sense of compulsion to give advice. It is also liberating for the new copule to realize that they are now being treated as they have been told they would be through life—as fully-fledged adults!

Children are to be obedient and honoring throughout their younger years, but when they become adults, they must remember that the honoring is still to continue throughout their lives. Honoring means sincerely listening to and willingly knowing what was stated, but knowing full well that there is no obligation on the child's part to follow the advice once it has been completely heard.

Parents are given the wonderful, awesome, and overwhelming responsibility to rear their children as God would have them reared. It is now time to pray with and enjoy your children as they continue in that which they have been taught. They will undoubtedly do things differently, and may even vacillate in what they do from decision to decision. They are simply trying to do what they believe to be best. In so doing, and if allowed to make their own decision, they may make their own mistakes. Allow them the privilege to do so. They will follow their own convictions, and in that, will understand better how to know and follow an even better authority—God!

There may be times the child will rebel and not follow God's truths—they may even walk away from the belief system they have been taught all their younger years. Parents still must recognize their children are adults and treat them as such. Praying for their salvation and submission to God is critical. They are at this time, however, no longer their child's authority.

Rear Them to Leave

When children are born into the family, parents should desire to rear them to leave them in a proper and mature manner. The safest place for anyone, a child included, is right in the center of God's will. To truly serve the Lord in spirit and truth (see John 4:24) is to desire from the outset to serve the Lord with one's life, wherever that may be. It is not right for parents to protect their children by keeping them dependent upon them. It should be their goal to help them be dependent upon God and independent of them.

The privilege of parenting doesn't stop when a child departs the home, but the immediate influence and necessity for the child to obey does cease. It is to that end that parents want to be sure their children have been reared to know God and want to love Him and serve Him for the rest of their lives. What the future holds may not be certain, but it is certain Who holds the future! Trusting in God while rearing children now translates into trusting God for their safekeeping during their independence to do all to the glory of the Lord.

Two Final Statements to Have Your Children Reflect On and Live By

The first is: It's not what a person can do that matters—it's what he or she should do! It is very easy to want to get to do what one pleases. Since God loves people enough to give them freedom of choices, then it will seem initially that they can do whatever isn't sin. Within that context, though, it is important to recognize that just because people *can* do something doesn't mean they *should.* Taking the long look, and recognizing that there are consequences for every action, will direct people to be certain they are doing what should be done.

Secondly: People may do anything they wish to do as long as God is pleased with it! At the outset, it will seem that this releases children to do whatever they want. As long as God is pleased with their choices, then that keeps them on track— and that is far more important than having them please either their parents or their peers. God should be the supreme choice in all aspects of life, and when children recognize that, and consistently pursue that with their whole heart, God will be pleased, and they will be blessed.

* * *

It's apparent you are a parent. You are a part of God's program to replenish the earth and to fill its nations with worshipers of the one, true and living God. And one day, your children will themselves be blessed and challenged in becoming parents. May the God of all grace give you and them wonderful success in following His precepts and being conformed to the likeness of

His Son, the Lord Jesus Christ, as you endeavor to do all things to His glory!

This compilation of data is, of course, from one person's perspective. I have sought throughout my years of parenting to seek God's wisdom. When relying upon my own wisdom and strength, I have failed on many occasions. When I have sought to follow God's plan and His principles, it has brought clarity and truth to proper parenting principles. I encourage you to seek God's will and way as you parent, and base all of your practices upon His Word rather than upon someone else's example or resource. It's tremendous to know that the blessing of seeking God is finding Him, and, while parenting, He Himself is the most valuable resource! May the Lord grant you His grace and truth as you parent for His glory!

Postscript

Off to a Bad Start? Don't Give Up!

P erhaps you are reading this book and you have not gotten off to a good start parenting scripturally. Now you are realizing, as Proverbs 13:12 states: "Hope deferred makes the heart sick." Unfulfilled expectations can be discouraging. Parents must continue to follow through with God's Word, realizing that whatever wrong has been done can, through God's help, be corrected. In Proverbs 13:19, Solomon says, "A desire fulfilled is sweet to the soul," revealing that parents can change their focus and patterns to what would please God as they bring up their children in the nurture and admonition of the Lord.

By God's grace and in His strength, you can still make the right changes!

Study guide

Chapter One

1. What qualifies you to *be* a parent?
2. What qualifies you to *parent*?
3. How can James 1:5 be such a comfort to parents?
4. Why does showing true commitment and kindness help in parenting?
5. What is the goal of parenting?
6. Why is it helpful to discuss the purpose of your parenting?
7. Why is it helpful to discuss any preconditioned expectations of parenting?
8. Why must parents agree upon and base their expectations upon scriptural principles?
9. How do parents adjust their initial expectations of parenting?
10. Why is focusing on Christ, and His pattern, so important in the parenting process?

Chapter Two

1. What is a supreme goal of parenting?
2. Why is it so important that parents reveal the goal of parenting on a personal level?
3. What is it going to take to rear a child to serve and please the Lord?

4. Why is Samuel such a great example of a person being influenced with truth?
5. Why is the human element such an obstacle in child-rearing?
6. Consider all the scriptural principles taught in this chapter and consider how you will implement them in your child-rearing.
    - Psalm 37:4
    - Proverbs 18:24 (KJV)
    - Matthew 5:3, 4, 5, 6, 7, 8, 11, 16–20, 37
    - Matthew 6:33; 7:7
    - Luke 6:30–36; 10:27
    - Ephesians 4:15, 16, 26, 32
    - Ephesians 6:1, 2
    - Philippians 2:3
    - Colossians 3:23
    - 1 Thessalonians 5:16–19
    - 1 Peter 1:16b

Chapter Three

1. What is a disciple?
2. What is obedience?
3. When it comes to obedience, what is the first step in following after God?
4. In parenting, what is the absolute standard?
5. How does the example of Saul's disobedience direct us toward obedience?
6. How does the example of Abraham's obedience direct us toward obedience?

7. What are the four qualities of true obedience?
8. How does each quality stand alone in its directives?
9. How does each quality relate to the other qualities of obedience?
10. What are the three overriding rules for your family?
11. What are the three overriding rules for child-rearing?
12. What is an appeal process? Why is it so helpful?

Chapter Four

1. Why is shepherding a child's heart so important?
2. Why is peace and calm a by-product of obedience?
3. For expectations to be realized, what must occur?
4. What is the motivation for discipline?
5. What are some important considerations in discipline?
6. Why should one establish ahead of time the basis for disciplining children?
7. Why should one establish ahead of time the standard implements for administering discipline?
8. Why should one establish a standard place to administer discipline?
9. Why should one establish a standard discipline policy?
10. Why should one establish ahead of time that he or she will always stay in control while disciplining?
11. Why should one establish ahead of time he or she will speak the truth in love, whether during discipline or casual conversation?
12. Why should one establish ahead of time reconciliation procedures?

Chapter Five

1. Why is a dad's influence of servant-leadership so important?
2. What is one ability in child-rearing to be desired above all others?
3. Why is it so important parents are disciplined themselves?
4. Why is following through with promises so important?
5. How does Deuteronomy 6:6–7 help parents today in their daily living and disciplining?
6. How can parents be living examples before their children?
7. Why is attitude so important?
8. Why is it so important to be able to "get away" from your children periodically?
9. What is a very important rule for your marriage and family? Why?
10. Why is being a role model so important?

Chapter Six

1. What are the characteristics of the telling phase, and which age is associated with this?
2. What are the characteristics of the instruction phase, and which age is associated with this?
3. What are the characteristics of the participating phase, and which age is associated with this?
4. What are the characteristics of the empowering phases and which age is associated with this?
5. What are the two important principles of modesty?
6. What is so important about rearing college and adult children?
7. Why is it so important to rear your children to leave?

8. What are the final two statements so important to leave with your children?
9. How does the teaching of Proverbs 13:12 affect parenting?
10. How does the teaching of Proverbs 13:19 affect parenting?